ALZE Steve Sinclair

# QUIVER'S CHOICE

*By the same author*

SAGITTARIUS RHYMING
LONDON WATCHES
TARGETS

# QUIVER'S CHOICE

*by*

SAGITTARIUS

JONATHAN CAPE
THIRTY BEDFORD SQUARE
LONDON

FIRST PUBLISHED 1945

JONATHAN CAPE LTD.   30 BEDFORD SQUARE, LONDON
AND 91 WELLINGTON STREET WEST, TORONTO

BOOK
PRODUCTION
WAR ECONOMY
STANDARD

THIS BOOK IS PRODUCED IN COM-
PLETE CONFORMITY WITH THE
AUTHORIZED ECONOMY STANDARDS

PRINTED IN GREAT BRITAIN IN THE CITY OF OXFORD
AT THE ALDEN PRESS
BOUND BY A. W. BAIN & CO. LTD., LONDON

# ACKNOWLEDGMENTS

MOST of these verses have been published in *The New Statesman and Nation* signed Sagittarius, in *Time and Tide* signed Fiddlestick and in *Tribune* signed Roger Service. The author's thanks are due to the Editors for permission to reprint.

# CONTENTS

## 1943-45

7

9

11

# 1943 — 45

## DAMP SQUIB

### Government Statement on Beveridge Social Security Plan

Tell it on the air,
Tell it oversea,
Britain will prepare
Planned security.
Tell it in the street,
Pass the happy news,
Tell it to the Fleet,
Tell it to the crews,
Tell it to the crowd,
Tell it to the groups,
Now it is allowed.
Tell it to the troops.
Spread it east and west,
Shout it south and north,
Set all doubts at rest,
Let the word go forth.
All can not be done
At a single bound,
But when peace is won,
If the means are found,
If we can regain
Our industrial lead,
And at home restrain
Injudicious speed,
If we hold our own
In our export trade,
When the cost is known,
When the risks are weighed,

If our burden's eased,
If our income rise,
If we have appeased
Private enterprise,
If we plan to do
What we can afford,
Leaving details to
A Statutory Board,
Backing social aims,
Straining every nerve,
Meeting public claims
With a wise reserve,
Let us rest content,
Sometime, if we can,
We shall implement
Half the Beveridge Plan.


## PERISH THE THOUGHT

The principal obstacle to the Dakar Fleet sailing out to the Atlantic and striking a blow at the U-boats appears to be barnacles. — *Daily Express*, January 12th.

Everyone spread alarmist versions,
Everyone guessed what the cause might be
When, in spite of Allied exertions,
French ships failed to put to sea.
Everyone knew the Fleet was free,
Everyone cried 'Perfidious Gaul!'
Now we take back such base aspersions —
It was barnacles after all.

Dangerous rumour and idle chatter,
Hints of shirking and compromise,
Seeds of baseless suspicion scatter —
Careless gossip may cost Allies.
Misunderstandings must then arise
Looming up like a Chinese Wall,
When we are told what was the matter —
It was barnacles after all.

Muzzle slander and gag suspicion,
Evil forces are not in play
Though at home we await transition
To the rainbow dawn of a brighter day.
Far from the facts our fancies stray
If plotting Tories our minds appal —
Now let us make the frank admission,
It is barnacles after all.

Every ship of State has got 'em,
Every Service Department too;
Barnacles hide, but when we spot 'em
Everyone knows the thing to do.
Drag the barnacles into view,
Give the vessel an overhaul —
Scrape the barnacles off the bottom,
What are barnacles, after all?

# RELIEF PRIORITY

The official British attitude towards sending food supplies into the unoccupied countries remains unchanged. — Report in *Manchester Guardian*.

If no relief may pass through our blockade
To Allied lands where children starve and die,
If no exception can for these be made,
If their last hope of rescue we deny
For fear provision for their need conveyed
Might give assistance to the enemy,
If our self-preservation must dictate
We leave a generation to its fate,

If in this cause we cannot now relent
Lest it should mean our adversary's gain,
How then did we the selfsame risk prevent
When shipments were allowed to ports of Spain,
Or when from Africa the convoys went
Which might the Axis war machine sustain,
And how then did we guard against the chance
The foe might be relieved through Vichy France?

If it were madness now, how was it wise,
Relaxing our restrictions, to permit
A flow of war material and supplies
For neutral Italy's sole benefit,
And what precautions did we then devise
That Germany should make no use of it?
How could it be we were less fearful then,
The foe being stronger both in arms and men?

If our embargo may be raised no more,
If they go hungry still, who might be fed,
Victims and sacrifices in our war,
So many doomed to die, so many dead,
However loudly we their fate deplore,
Let us consider well, lest it be said
Our words ring false, our action ever tends
Rather to buy our foes than save our friends.


# THE FRIGHTENING FRENCH

Marcel Peyrouton was last night officially announced as the new
Governor-General of Algeria . . . it is the worst choice that could have
been made. Peyrouton is distrusted by Frenchmen of all parties,
detested by the Arab population and loathed by de Gaulle and his
colleagues. — *Daily Herald*, January 20th.

When France under Pétain's control
Her pact of dishonour completed,
Great Britain joined hands with de Gaulle
And the Free French fought on, undefeated.
De Gaulle whom the foe could not buy
Then saved Fighting France from despair —
*Nous avons perdu une bataille!*
*Nous n'avons pas perdu la guerre!*

When Darlan bade Frenchmen unite,
Before his appropriate removal,
He called to the ex-Vichyite,
Assured of the Allies' approval.
Algiers offers jobs in profusion,
But Fighting French need not apply;
If we fought for de Gaullists' inclusion
*Nous avons perdu la bataille.*

As the generals instal in his place
The Admiral's fitting successor
The cause of free men we disgrace
By appointing Tunisia's oppressor.
Though we fight as Democracy's saviour
We give Fascists a snug pied-à-terre —
All traitors to France are in favour —
*Les gens qui ont perdu la guerre.*

Giraud still remains on the scene,
But since Giraud is no politician,
With a record so curiously clean
How can he retain his position?
In Algiers under our occupation
The sun of the Fascists rides high,
And though it's but for the duration
*De Gaulle a perdu la bataille.*

And what though our armies advance,
Sweeping on to a victory glorious,
If the Allies desert Fighting France
By appeasing appeasers notorious,
If Vichy must be our ally,
If Free Frenchmen are given no share,
*Nous aurons gagné les batailles,*
*Mais nous aurons perdu la guerre.*


## THE GLOBULE

Global war and global peace,
Global measures for lend-lease;
Nothing now delays the plan
But the birth of Global Man.

# LET'S BE FAIR

Mr. Macmillan asked correspondents not to be harsh with former Vichy followers in the government, reminding them that there is a lot of difference between a traitor and one of the weaker brethren who choose the path of least resistance. — *Evening Standard*, February 8th.

Don't be harsh with Peyrouton
For a past mistake,
Do not criticize Boisson,
Give Bergeret a break.

Don't refer to them as crooks,
Renegades and twisters,
Don't keep them in your bad books,
Vichy's non-resisters.

Don't charge them with treachery
Though they played with traitors,
Don't forget they still may be
Good administrators.

While they do not represent
France's underground
It is amply evident
All of them are sound.

Now that they have turned again,
Give the gang a chance,
Let these weaker brethren
Speak for fighting France.

All war criminals will face
Trials stern but just,
Save those quislings whom we place
In offices of trust.

Though they once were followers
In Pétain's Old Guard,
Now they're Giraud's Ministers,
Please, please, don't be hard.


# COMMERCIAL TRAVELLERS

We want . . . greatly improved consular services, equipped not only
to analyse markets abroad . . . but ready to collaborate with industry's
representatives and customers on the spot. — Mr. H. Morrison,
February 14th.

Our envoys may no longer shine,
Heirs to a diplomatic line
And proud tradition.
His Excellency's beams are shorn,
His wasted talents must adorn
A business mission;
Renouncing his Imperial creed
He barters with the lesser breed.

Democracy's Ambassador
For export trade need be no more
A titled person.
O phantoms of a vanished day!
O Crewe! O Salisbury! O Grey!
O shade of Curzon!
It is a task no longer ours
To hold the scales between the Powers.

Can we past influence renew
With sovereignties allergic to
Our world examples?
No more.  Once arbiter of kings,
To-day His Excellency brings
A case of samples.
Othello's occupation's gone
But customers are waited on.

The tactics of the tête-à-tête,
Skill in manœuvres delicate
And confidential,
The exercise of brilliant tact,
The technique of the secret pact,
Are not essential.
Compelled his courtly role to drop
His Excellency keeps a shop.

No more by methods indirect
Can he great Powers or small infect
With Anglomania.
Farewell the old diplomacy!
Farewell finesse! a long good-bye
To Ruritania.
Gone with the wind his past prestige,
He stoops to trade. *Noblesse oblige!*

# PEACE AIMS

There has been a good deal of what might almost be called humbug about much of this post-war oratory. — *Manchester Guardian*, February 27th.

The nations of the Grand Alliance,
 Their separate interests kept in mind,
Proclaim unqualified compliance
 With plans for bettering mankind.

Engaged to carry to fruition
 The promise of the age of gold,
They waive imperialist ambition —
 But what they have they mean to hold.

Old systems fighting for survival,
 With progress still wage endless feud
While each pretends the rest to rival
 In projects for the common good.

Habituated to disguise,
 The spokesman of united nations
Their aims omit to advertise,
 And only tell their aspirations.

# DEAR LADIES

The value of women in the (Foreign) Service does not depend upon the value set upon them in this country, but on the reception they would receive in foreign countries ... there are 28 countries where it would be impossible to send women. — Mr. Law, Under-Secretary, Foreign Office, March 18th.

You are knocking at the Foreign Office door,
Dear ladies,
You remind us of your service in the war,
Dear ladies;
You are cherishing some notion
Of reward for your devotion,
But promotion is no nearer than before.

In eight-and-twenty sadly backward lands,
Dear ladies,
Where woman follows and where man commands,
Dear ladies,
It would lead to complications,
And give rise to protestations
If the nation's interests rested in your hands.

We pray you will not raise a teacup storm,
Dear ladies,
If to foreign prejudice we must conform,
Dear ladies;
Though countries more enlightened
By your presence would be brightened,
We are frightened others might be quite lukewarm.

25

The fair ambassadress might well be tried,
Dear ladies,
If she had a British husband by her side,
Dear ladies,
But we deprecate romances,
For, if natives make advances,
There are chances she'd become an alien's bride.

You can help your husbands on in their career,
Dear ladies,
But alas, in our high diplomatic sphere,
Dear ladies,
Use of female intuition
Leads to failure of a mission,
Your ambition cannot be encouraged here.

We fear we cannot fruitfully discuss,
Dear ladies,
A proposition so ridiculous,
Dear ladies,
Though we trust we show quite clearly
We admire your gifts sincerely,
You must really leave diplomacy to us.


## ALL ROADS LEAD TO ROME

Peacemakers take the road to Rome as signs of doom increase
To guard against the chance of revolutionary peace,
They may plead for intercession as the Church's faithful sons —
But Rome can hear from Africa the thunder of the guns.

The peace plans of the Axis have no prospect of success,
But how different the proposal that the Vatican may bless,
Then the faithful in democracies might readily agree —
But Rome can feel a tremor from the shores of Sicily.

When the Axis is defeated Rome may yet save Europe's soul
If the Fascists can be rescued from the wreckage of the whole;
Rome might yet preserve the quislings and the regents and the kings —
But from Spezia and Naples Rome can hear the beat of wings.

They are drowning in the Deluge and the road to Rome is dark,
All Europe's under water and the Vatican's the Ark,
So the road to Rome is crowded and peace kites begin to fly —
But Rome is looking upward at the lightning in the sky.

The visiting Archbishops and the papal diplomats
Are sending out the doves of peace to find their Ararats,
They are loosed above the waters but they cannot find a home,
And Rome has heard Montgomery is on the road to Rome.

## THE PLAN TO END THE PLAN

### *After G. K. Chesterton*

The Five Year Plan of the Soviet State was a sharing plan, an unsparing
    plan,
A ruthlessly overbearing plan to persons with land and gold,
Which propagated a point of view essentially proletarian
With agriculture and industry exclusively state-controlled.
But we will fashion a Tory plan,
And a Liberal plan and a Labour plan,
A master plan for the Empire State
Of no class or party type,
A plan for trade and a plan for aid,
But not a beggar-my-neighbour plan
Which anti-planners can formulate
As soon as the time is ripe.

27

Roosevelt's New Deal was a Four Year Plan, a productive plan, an
    instructive plan,
A lifeline thrown to the little man when the bosses had come to grief,
But the N.R.A. of Washington could hardly be called a seductive plan
To Democrats or Republicans who were not on State relief.
But we will frame a protection plan,
An export trade resurrection plan,
A plan for private enterprise
And a plan for public health,
A spacious plan, a capacious plan,
A bumper General Election plan,
A plan of fruitful compromise
And a plan for vested wealth.


The Four Year Plan of the German Reich was a furious plan, a
    penurious plan,
Which regimented the common man while the living standard fell,
A vicious plan, a pernicious plan, a very highly injurious plan,
And a plan that failed to find the means for butter and guns as well.
But we will make a defensive plan,
A wider and more comprehensive plan,
A plan to leave things as they are
If planners would interfere;
With each advance backed by sound finance
It won't be a too-expensive plan,
And a plan that does not go too far
Is a plan for sober cheer.


The Uthwatt, Scott and Beveridge plans are romantic plans and
    pedantic plans
They are plans to fight against owners' rights in property and land,
But these can all be safely merged in wider and more gigantic plans
Where half is planned for the general good and half may remain
    unplanned.

We will not have an autarchic plan,
An ideologic, anarchic plan,
Plans taking a class or a party line
Will find few partisans,
Our domestic plan, a majestic plan
Will be simply and solely Churchillian —
A plan where all of the plans combine
Is a Plan to End the Plans.


# WHAT WILL THEY USE FOR MONEY?

If sacrificial taxes spread a Budgetary gloom,
Life is brightened by the prospect of a post-war trading boom
As the charter of prosperity the British public scan
In the Treasury White Paper (or the Washington White Plan).

One a Fund for stabilizing
One a Union for clearing,
Both are plans for energizing,
Both to debtor nations cheering;
One in Bancor makes advances,
One's with Unitas provided,
Each will manage world finances,
Which has not yet been decided.

Nations with diminished credit and with commerce moribund
May be members of the Union (or shareholders in the Fund)
Qualified by credit quotas on Keynes' Bancor Bank to draw
(Or through Unitas to borrow from the hoard of Morgenthau).

The White Paper's staunch supporters
Claim the Keynes' Plan is the right plan,
While New York's financial quarters
Are insistent on the White Plan.

Debtor States at the proposal
Do not share the experts' rancour —
They will have at their disposal
Either Unitas or Bancor.

While experiencing shortages in shillings, pounds and pence,
Gifts of Unitas (or Bancor) seem a bounteous Providence,
And once Wall Street and Threadneedle Street their differences adjust,
World finance will be conducted in a burst of mutual trust.

Then the Fund will be promoted
As the Banker of the nations
(Or the Union will be voted
To control price fluctuations)
Each with monetary units as
A currency sheet-anchor,
Which either will be Unitas,
Or alternatively, Bancor.

## BERMUDA

*[After Andrew Marvell]*

Where the remote Bermudas ride
The refugees' lost cause is tried —
The Conference records its grief
That it can offer no relief.
Now from that hospitable coast
Where once (of which they rather boast)
Faith's martyrs in an earlier age
Escaped from persecution's rage,
Two nations, as they bar the gate
To victims of the Nazi's hate,
Recite, their action to explain,
This noble (but uncheerful) strain.

'The persecuted with one voice
At coming victory rejoice,
When the oppressors we'll expel,
And free the slaves (the Jews as well).
While sanctuary we begrudge,
The executioners we judge,
And here repeat that monstrous crime
Earns retribution; but meantime
The problem is too mighty grown
For our democracies alone.
We do not solely hold the keys
To open doors to refugees.
In war we must decline to give
Admission to the fugitive,
Nor to this meeting can invite
The lesser neutral states who might.
United nations have done much
To save souls from the hangman's clutch
And at this session we explore
The reasons we can do no more.
And while a race, it is presumed,
Is to extermination doomed,
With victory we'll not refuse
Asylum to surviving Jews.
Let none be by false hopes betrayed,
Or clamour for immediate aid,
But let us here our cause exalt,
Till our song soars to Heaven's vault.'

Where the Bermudas ride remote
This noble (but uncheerful) note,
Voice of inaction and delay,
Echoes beyond the Mexique Bay,
(From whence a more inviting strain
Welcomes Republicans from Spain),

And may (perhaps) be heard afar
In Poland's streaming abattoir,
Where (doubtless) those about to die,
Would (were it possible) reply,
Approving of the long-term plans
Of would-be good Samaritans.


## COTTAGE IN THE AIR

In the House of Commons Mr. De la Bere asked the Prime Minister whether, in view of the fact that at the present time four or more Ministries are interested in, and dealing with, the proposals for the erection of farm cottages for agricultural workers, he will give an assurance that effective co-ordination is being maintained, in view of the urgent national necessity for the speedy erection of these cottages?

Three thousand token cottage homes
On sites of rustic charm,
Were planned to house, come harvest time,
Our agricultural arm;
First fruits of building policy
To meet an urgent need,
Sign of official energy
And Departmental speed.

The M.O.A.'s State cottages
Appeared upon the plan,
The M.O.W. rounded off
What the M.O.H. began;
But the M.O.S. and M.O.L.
Refused priority,
And the cottage homes were pigeon-holed
For the M.O.T.C.P.

The Rural District Councils soon
Reported with alarm
The dearth of suntrap cottages
For workers on the farm —
No cottages come Lady Day,
None by Midsummer's date;
Come harvest-home, come Michaelmas,
Come Christmas, they were late.

Nor, yet come Doomsday will they build
Three thousand shadow cotts.
(With all mod. con. and comf. accomm.
For agricultural tots)
Till the M.O.W., M.O.A.,
And M.O.H. agree
With M.O.S., and M.O.L.
And M.O.T.C.P.


## AGINCOURT FRONT

Regarding the filming in Technicolour of Henry V . . . the Agincourt battle scenes are to be 'shot' in Eire. Only there can many hun-
dreds of stalwart men be available to act as supers. — News item,
*Manchester Guardian.*

Once more rehearse the scene, good Celts, once more
Let English-Irish lay French-Irish low!
Now think the blast of war blows in your ears
And imitate the action of belligerents;
Stiffen your sinews, think once more of Cromwell,
And so comport yourselves as English yeomen,
That Nazi agents now at work in Dublin
May count them happy you are not their foes!
Think, as you fright the air in County Wicklow,
You sweep the very field of Agincourt!

On, on, you kerns and gallowglasses, on,
Advance, you stout Sinn Feiners, brawny supers
Whose limbs were made in Eire, show us here
That you are worth your wages: which I doubt not,
Are ten times more than those of Harry's bowmen!
And he that doth enact this scene with me,
Let him be never so Republican
He is this day King Harry's follower!
On to the charge! though there is none of you
But hath a neutral lustre in his eye,
And say, this day I act an Englishman!
Now set the teeth, hold hard the breath, and strike!
Follow your leader, and upon your cue
Charge for St. Patrick and the Emerald Isle!


# UTHWATT AND SCOTT
## [*After Edward Lear*]

Lord Selborne's statement that Ministers had no time at present to
consider the question of forming a policy for the future must have left
the House with a gloomy impression of the Government's attitude
towards the whole process of reconstruction. — *The Times*, May 31st.

The Government's firmness is open to doubt
When interim plans are debated without
a SHOT
At Uthwatt and Scott.

Will the Cabinet shortly their viewpoint disclose,
Will they back them in principle, will they oppose
a LOT
Of Uthwatt and Scott?

Will the Ministries rule upon rebuilding sites,
Will the Government lease land development rights
                    or NOT
                    Through Uthwatt and Scott?

Does the Cabinet favour long-term schemes or short?
Will the property owners endeavour to thwart
                    by a PLOT
                    Both Uthwatt and Scott?

Will land speculation be strictly controlled,
Is the Government attitude tepid or cold
                    or HOT,
                    Towards Uthwatt and Scott?

Will both be put on ice like the Beveridge Plan,
Will they simply pass over, or actively ban,
                    or NOT,
                    Both Uthwatt and Scott?

Will these far-reaching recommendations be tried,
Or will the proposals be all set aside
                    or FORGOT,
                    Of Uthwatt and Scott?

Are their prospects uncertain or gloomy or bright,
Does the Cabinet think them a blessing, a blight
                    or a BLOT
                    Uthwatt and Scott?

Will they ever be pushed at a breakneck pace,
Will reconstruction gallop or race
                    or TROT,
                    With Uthwatt and Scott?

Will they stand as a basis for legislation
Or be left in suspended animation
                                        to ROT,
                              Uthwatt and Scott?


# ANNO DOMINI, 1942

In Rama was there a voice heard, lamentation and weeping and
great mourning, Rachel weeping for her children, and would not be
comforted, because they are not. — St. Matthew.

Once from wicked Herod's city
Fled a Mother with her Son,
Sheltered in the land of Egypt
Till the tyrant's course was run.
Not the Queen of Heaven was she,
But a Jewish refugee.

Though in times of pagan darkness
Slaughter of the innocents
Was not met with solemn protests
By humaner governments,
Exiles in the realm of Caesar
Did not need a transit visa.

Now two thousand years have followed,
Blessing Man with milder rule,
Once more Israel's children perish
But to-day the world is full.
Earth is full, there is no room
For Israel in Christendom.

Only in the place of slaughter
None need for admittance wait,
Death does not restrict the quota,
All may enter at his gate;
But they nail the *Keep Out* sign
At the gate of Palestine.

Milk of human kindness flowing,
Warmth of Christian charity,
In the modern Herod's shambles
Israel's children will not see.
Sanctuary there is none
For the mother nor the son.


## HOT NEWS FROM HOT SPRINGS

Once starvation has been prevented ... emphasis will shift to the
elimination of gross deficiencies of diet ... ensuring subsistence for
every man, woman and child in India, China and Africa. — *The Times.*

The welfare and health of the world commonwealth
Is a challenge to planners' sagacity,
But the experts conclude that they rest upon food
And depend on stomachic capacity.
The glut and the shortage, the slump and the boom
Will always give cause for disquiet
Till Asia and Africa learn to consume
An ample yet minimum diet.

Food facts must be known in the tropical zone,
For they plan on the hopeful presumption
That global production for world reconstruction
Will be balanced by global consumption.

The era of plenty we cannot expect,
Nor make freedom from want a reality,
Till the underfed races are taught to reject
Their time-honoured cult of frugality.

Flesh, fat and proteins, fish, cereals and beans
Every man must be ready to swallow,
Grain, starches and fruits, seeds, tubers and roots,
With leguminous items to follow.
Bananas and yams must no longer suffice,
Nut-eating gives reason for worry,
Nor must natives persist in a diet of rice
With occasional sprinklings of curry.

The mild overeating prescribed by this meeting
Can solve the world's ills economic,
And they see no resistance to standard subsistence
Except from some cause anatomic.
The Conference therefore to mankind appeals
To get down to the job with tenacity —
All must learn to sit fast and face up to their meals,
And enlarge their stomachic capacity.

## QUARREL SCENE

SCENE: *A tent in Algiers.* GENERAL DE GAULLE *discovered, sulking.*

(*Enter* GENERAL GIRAUD)

GIRAUD    General, I say that you have done me wrong.
DE GAULLE    I only deal with written grievances.
GIRAUD    You do not answer letters; I will speak.
DE GAULLE    If you speak softly we will give you audience.

| | |
|---|---|
| GIRAUD | And who may 'we' be, General de Gaulle? |
| DE GAULLE | We are the President. 'L'Etat, c'est moi!' |
| GIRAUD | We are co-Presidents. 'L'Etat, c'est nous!' |
| | That you have wronged me must appear in this — |
| | You are conspiring to usurp my place. |
| DE GAULE | I am elected your superior. |
| GIRAUD | Shall I give way to one of lesser rank? |
| | I am commander. |
| DE GAULLE | Under my command. |
| GIRAUD | Try me no more, I shall forget myself. |
| | It was agreed the Army should be mine. |
| DE GAULLE | Let me remind you *I* did not agree: |
| | Do not presume too much upon our patience. |
| GIRAUD | Ye gods, Ye gods, must I endure all this? |
| | Remember, General, to whom you speak; |
| | Last Friday Catroux asked us both to tea, |
| | Which I indeed accepted on conditions, |
| | But you declined, although no soldier may |
| | Refuse to meet a senior officer. |
| DE GAULLE | I *can* refuse to, as co-President. |
| GIRAUD | On Saturday Catroux bade us to luncheon, |
| | Once more you slighted off the invitation. |
| DE GAULLE | I would not lunch with you, though ten times begged, |
| | I warn you, General, try me not too high, |
| | For if you drive me to it, I'll resign. |
| GIRAUD | Do so, and bay the moon in Brazzaville. |
| DE GAULLE | And leave the field to you? No, by the Gods! |
| GIRAUD | I thought you would not, and that being so, |
| | There is no terror in your idle threats. |
| DE GAULLE | Take care. The Empire waits my word to rise. |
| GIRAUD | That will be news in Syria and Dakar. |
| DE GAULLE | The populace of Algiers cheers for me. |
| GIRAUD | Algerian summer is too hot for you, |
| | I urged our meeting in a calmer place. |
| DE GAULLE | It is for you Algiers will be too hot. |

GIRAUD    Let us return to the Catroux affair.
                    (GENERAL CATROUX, *within*)
CATROUX   Let me go and see the Generals.  There is some grudge
               between them.
                    (*Enter* GENERAL CATROUX)
               The National Committee begs from you
               Some public pledge of Frenchmen's unity.
DE GAULLE But know you not there are no Frenchmen now?
               All are de Gaullists, or else Giraudists.
CATROUX   I shall remember, and advise them of it.
DE GAULLE Wait, I'll go with you.  I preside to-day.
GIRAUD    To-morrow is your turn; to-day is mine.
DE GAULLE Give place, I take the chair.  Tell them, Catroux.
CATROUX   Why not both come, both being Presidents?
GIRAUD    You have your orders.  Let me pass, de Gaulle.
CATROUX   If there are slight adjustments still to make
               Before the meeting you will come to tea?
DE GAULLE General Catroux, you do deny your oath,
               As a de Gaullist, to invite Giraud.
GIRAUD    And I have in concessions gone too far
               Not for the world will I take tea with you.
               I shall preside to-day.  Out of my path!
CATROUX   But soft, here comes an Allied messenger.
                    (*Enter a* MESSENGER *with a dispatch.* GIRAUD *and* DE
                    GAULLE *both reach for it.* CATROUX *takes it, and reads*)
               Generals de Gaulle and Giraud will take tea
               With General Eisenhower, K.C.B.

# MEIN GOODNESS! MEIN FORTRESS!

## [*After 'Erlkönig', by Goethe*]

Hitler has just returned from a visit to his birthplace . . . it is assumed
he wished to get away from the influence of his military chiefs and
recover the state of free-mindedness which he used to seek in the
days when he had successful intuitions. — 'Inside Information', *Daily
Sketch*, June 23rd.

Who races so fast through tempest and storm?
It's the Führer pursuing a beckoning form;
Over rubble and ruin his footsteps are led
While his bright Intuition keeps two jumps ahead.

'Mein Führer, mein Führer, why do you turn pale?
Come follow, come fly through the blast and the gale,
The vision of victory dawns on my view,
I can hardly describe what is coming to you!

'Your genius burns brightly, your strategy's plain,
And destiny smiles on your global campaign,
Your *Volk* are so trustful, your fortress secure!'
'But can't you hear something go *crump* in the Ruhr?'

'To eastward, to eastward your *Lebensraum* lies,
To Moscow! to Moscow! it falls by surprise!
You have only to name the victorious day!'
'But don't you see something that stands in the way?'

'To Cairo, to Suez, divert the attack,
The feeble Eighth Army will certainly crack!'
'Mein goodness, mein goodness, I tried that before,
But where and O where is mein Afrika Korps?'

'To England! To England! Her end is at hand!
The Wehrmacht awaits your decisive command.
One last blitz on London, and all will be won!'
'But where is mein beautiful Luftwaffe gone?'

'Mein Führer, mein Führer, you're lagging behind.'
'I must pause to recapture my freedom of mind.'
'Come follow, fly faster, this place is too hot!'
'Mein goodness! mein fortress! mein Axis! mein Gott!'


## WAS IT REALLY NECESSARY?

War alone brings all human energy to the highest tension and puts
the stamp of nobility on peoples with courage to meet it. — Mussolini.

What did the Fascists cry?
Glorious war!
What did Fate prophesy?
Victorious war!
Italy's destiny,
Stamp of virility,
Symbol of victory,
Glorious war!
Now the invaders strike
Italy's shore,
Fascists seem not to like
Glorious war.
Doubts will come creeping in,
Can Fascists save their skin?
Can anti-Fascists win
Glorious war?
What was the Fascist task?
Nothing but war!

What did the Fascists ask?
                    Only for more,
Only to write their name
First on the scroll of fame —
Now it is not the same
                    Glorious war.
What brings the Fascists down?
                    Glorious war!
Empire, State and Crown,
                    Glorious war!
Now the Allies attack,
What drives the legions back,
What makes the Fascists crack?
                    Glorious war!
Loudly Il Duce cries
                    Glorious war!
Gayda alone replies
                    'Glorious war!'
Now they are being hit
Fascists appear to quit —
They've had enough of it,
                    Glorious war!


## THE LITTLE DUKE

BEVIN  Young lad, come forth; I have to say with you.

(*Enter the* LITTLE DUKE)

DUKE  Good-morrow, Bevin.

BEVIN                          Good morning, little duke.

DUKE  Great heavens, Bevin, how you frown on me!
        Is it my fault my father was a peer?
        Indeed is't not.

BEVIN (*showing a paper*) Read here, young gentleman.
(*Aside*)
I must deal sternly with him, lest my colleagues
Think that I waver in my resolution —
They are afraid of me and I of them.

DUKE What, must I be conscripted for the mines?

BEVIN I said 'directed' not 'conscripted', duke.
Our shrinking man-power must be supplemented
By the boy-power of the community,
Without distinction as to class or rank.

DUKE Alas, the Minister of Fuel and Power
Said only last week, he had closed the gap.

BEVIN Major Lloyd George was grossly misinformed.

DUKE But must you do't? I will economize,
Eat dinner raw, and never light a fire,
I'll take a two-inch bath but once a se'nnight. . . .

BEVIN Go to, and hold your tongue. This childish prate
Gives me a headache.

DUKE                                    Have you a headache, Bevin?
In sooth, I think you look a little sick.

BEVIN Tut: take this paper and be off, young duke.

DUKE: O, mercy! I'll do almost anything —
Make me a soldier or a midshipman,
A District or B.B.C. Messenger,
Direct me to the Aircraft industry,
Drive me to some position in the City,
Set me to labour in the Foreign Office,
But save me, Bevin, save me from the mines.

BEVIN: There is no remedy.

DUKE:                                    What of rationing?

BEVIN: Ha, you have touched me on a tender spot.

44

DUKE: You have a tender spot! I knew it, Bevin.
Your heart is not of flint, and so to you
Your vile intent must needs seem horrible.
Ah, think for once it is a poor man's son,
And not a wretched peer who pleads with you,
Nay, if mine own Headmaster had come down
And told me that you contemplate this harm,
I'd not have believed him — no tongue but Bevin's.

BEVIN (*aside*): His innocent words do agitate my bosom —
Shall I be charged with class discrimination?
I am best pleased to put off such a deed.

(*Aloud*)

I will think further on my purpose, boy.
You are reprieved. Yet something must be done.

They will not take the miners from the ranks,
They cannot flog the miners in the pits —
But soft! I may conscript your grandmother,
And send her down the mine.

DUKE:                                    I thank thee, Ernie.

BEVIN: Tush, the decision does not rest with me.
'Tis Cabinet responsibility.
More headaches must I undergo for thee.

(*Exeunt*)

# COUNTRYSIDE CONTROL

*[After William Allingham]*

There should be an extension of organized visits officially recognized by the Board of Education of parties of children to the countryside. If educational publicity fails adequately to control the use of the countryside by the urban public, there should be stricter law enforcement. Bridle paths should be under the Footpaths Commission. — Scott Report.

Down the public footpath,
Through the right of way
We daren't go a-roving
Upon a holiday —
Fences round the hillside,
Railings round the heather,
Children of the green belt
Marching all together.

When the Lakes and moorlands
Become the nation's park
Look out for the keepers —
Gates shut after dark!
Read the regulations
If you hike or climb,
Learn the Chiltern curfew,
Skiddaw's closing time!
Authorized officials
Will urban persons guide
As to means of access
To the countryside.

High up in Whitehall
The Park Commission sits, —
They've been so long a-sitting
They've nigh lost their wits.

Rural District Councils
Plant warnings here and there
On the heaths and commons
'Trespassers Beware!'
If any man so daring
As pull them down in spite
He will find he's taken
To prison for the night

Up the scheduled mountain,
Down the earmarked glen,
The Board of Education
Is fanning out its men —
Urchins of the green belt
Rambling with the schools,
Youth Groups with their leaders,
Rambling by the rules,
Bye-laws on the hillside,
Fences round the heather,
Lovers and their lasses
Marching all together.


## GREAT RESIGNATIONS

Dictators seldom chuck their situation,
Few tyrants care to give themselves the sack,
Napoleon once resolved on abdication,
His crown renounced, and after snatched it back;
Old Diocletian is a classic sample
And Charles the Fifth gave up the daily grind,
Alfonso is a modern choice example,
And Mussolini also has resigned.

The sawdust Caesar, the new Machiavelli,
The Fascist version of the lion-heart
Who failed to armour-plate the underbelly
Of which he was himself the softest part;
The new Napoleon has got out from under
And will not have a chance to change his mind —
Great resignations are a nine-days' wonder,
And Mussolini also has resigned.

As doom inexorably forward marches
He recognizes that no fate ordains
That he should fight upon his fallen arches
To the last drop of sawdust in his veins.
With one great gesture of renunciation
He fades out, leaving not a wrack behind;
And with an even greater resignation,
Rome learns that Mussolini has resigned.

When Hitler's General Staff (or intuition)
Advise he should be put upon the shelf,
And when the Führer, in this strange position,
Must hand his resignation to himself,
The Chancellor may seek to use persuasion
But will recall, before it is declined,
The Kaiser crawled out on a like occasion,
And Mussolini also has resigned.

# ALIAS SIR GALAHAD

*[After Lord Tennyson]*

His right arm waves the goodly brand,
His right hand thrusteth sure,
The movements of his other hand
However, are obscure.
He frees the slave from shame and thrall,
His fighting arm is tough and strong,
The other is political
And near ten times as long.
So forth he fares and on he rides
Bedight in Anglo-U.S. mail;
He will not rest upon his quest
Until he finds the holy grail.


His right arm hath the foeman cleft
In many a shattering bout,
But still the conduct of his left
Full oft gives cause for doubt.
His right hand bears his broadsword clean,
His stainless armour is complete —
His left hand weaves a web unseen
Which trippeth up his feet.
And when his right has felled the foe
While paeans of neutral praise resound,
The self-same knight by left-hand sleight
He leadeth to the Table Round.


In Moscow and in Leningrad
They watch with interest
The exploits of Sir Galahad
Upon his two-way quest.

To them it seems what is to do
Is a two-handed enterprise,
And sometimes they express the view
That both should synchronize.
And as he wendeth on his way,
They darkly, in a glass perceive,
Though pure in heart he rides apart
And keepeth something up his sleeve.

And from each liberated spot
Strange rumours start to buzz,
Whether the knight's right arm can wot
That which his left arm does.
His strength is as the strength of ten,
He calls for casques to carve and crack,
Yet ever and anon again
His left hand holds him back.
All-armed he rides in helm and mail
And pricks along his devious route —
He will not fail to find the grail,
Or else a working substitute.


## THE TWO WARS

The Russian war is faster,
The Allied war is later,
Its execution vaster,
And its implications greater;
The Russian war is mobile
With a limited objective,
The Allied war is global,
Fitted in a world-perspective.

The Soviet offensive
Is expressed in operations,
The Allied, more extensive
Halts its march for conversations;
Their talks are periodic,
Their strategy is serial,
Their action episodic,
Their outlook is Imperial.

The Russians force decisions,
The Allies plan dispersal,
Postponing armed collisions
For a climax universal
The Red strokes are incessant,
Confined to one locality;
The Allies plan at present
For ultimate finality.

The Russian war is stiffer,
Its tempo is torrential,
The Reds and Allies differ
On the share of war potential:
The Allies work in unity
On courses contradictory,
The Reds ask opportunity
To stage an instant victory.

The Russian war is urgent
The Allied goal is distant,
With purposes divergent
Two wars are co-existent.
The Allies find admissible
A strategy one-sided —
Peace may be indivisible
But War can be divided.

# FORWARD

*[With apologies to the late Lord Tennyson]*

Rich in fulfilment unrevealed
Another Conference concludes,
The third of pregnant interludes
Between advances in the field.

Another plan of range immense,
Unfolding with majestic pace
And broadening from base to base,
From Conference to Conference.

Another talk each talk succeeds,
Of still more universal scope,
Enshrining yet more fervent hope,
One meeting to another leads;

For either on the heaving deck
Met on some favoured ocean site,
Or else upon the terraced height
Of Casablanca or Quebec,

Progressing with a widening view,
Itinerant from pole to pole,
A solar centre of control,
A migratory G.H.Q.,

Proceeding through the hemispheres
Through zones of brightness and of gloom,
In secrecy as of the tomb,
In unity too deep for tears,

As tasks of ever vaster scale
Demand more general debate,
Fraught with the load of sombre fate
Behind the veil, behind the veil,

World architects, war strategists,
They strive for mankind's utmost good,
To fuse in larger brotherhood
A world of isolationists,

Rolling along through destined grooves,
And train of cause and consequence
Towards that crowning Conference
To which the whole creation moves.

## THE LISBON STORY

'The Lisbon Story', as it came to be known among diplomats who shared its secrets, began in August when Italian approaches were made to British representatives in two neutral countries. — *News Chronicle*, September 13th.

How fascinating is the Lisbon story,
How true to type for secret service thrillers,
Clandestine talks on neutral territory
To snatch a victim from the Nazi killers.

What secret flights, what passwords, what disguises,
What guards against a diplomatic leak,
What taut suspense, what horrible surprises
For Nazi agents, playing hide and seek.

And how sensational the culmination,
When the Italians, in the victor's tent
In token of complete capitulation
Sign clauses which they cannot implement.

General Badoglio unifies resistance,
His fooled ex-Allies fall into the trap —
Premier Badoglio from the safest distance
Leaves his new followers to take the rap.

The battle Fleet that seldom fought, surrenders,
Vittorio and Badoglio see the light,
These are their people's nominal defenders —
(Or would be if they had not taken flight.)

While talks proceed the Allies' grip relaxes,
Milan is pounded in the common cause —
The head of the decapitated Axis
Turns to account the military pause.

The enemy is firmly in possession,
The Allies hail a diplomatic score,
The Lisbon Story makes a deep impression —
It is magnificent, but is it war?

# A WORD TO THE WISE

The Polish Government stands firm for the integrity of Polish
territory . . . we see no adequate reason why Poland should make any
further sacrifices, either in territory or in population. — Polish Foreign
Minister, September 13th.

> Poland, Great Britain stands beside you still,
> As we stood by you in your testing hour,
> Our solemn pledge by all means to fulfil
> Within our power.
>
> Sustained by your heroic fortitude,
> Concerting the annihilating blow,
> We stand to-day exactly where we stood
> Four years ago.
>
> Our sinews to the final onslaught bent,
> But still as impotent to intervene,
> Because the land mass of the Continent
> Still lies between.
>
> Steadfast as when we launched on total war
> That from your ruins you might rise again,
> We cannot now relieve you any more
> Than we could then.
>
> But pending our victorious advance
> You may, though prematurely, be released —
> The hammer-stroke of your deliverance
> Comes from the East.
>
> Though neither disappointment nor delay
> Can nip the hope we mutually nursed,
> Our great Ally, already on the way,
> Will reach you first.

Across the Donetz and beyond the Don,
Near Kiev and Smolensk your deliverers are
And soon to cross the Dnieper, driving on
The Vistula.

Poland may rule a Greater Poland yet,
Her soul exalted and her role sublime —
But make your peace now with the Soviet,
While there is time.


## LIPARI

The roaring Liberators fly
To set the captive peoples free.
The hawking Lightnings ride the sky,
Destroyers over Sicily.
They see the islands far beneath,
The fortress isles, the isle of death,
The penal isle of Lipari.

The shadow of the bomber's wing
Falls on the islands and the sea,
What hope, what promise do they bring,
Avengers over Sicily?
And do they come to liberate
The prisoners in chains, who wait
On long-forgotten Lipari?

The Flying Fortresses in might
Strike at the heart of Italy,
The Hurricanes sweep down in flight
On Corsica and Sicily;
But will they turn aside to save
The captives in their living grave —
The Devil's Isle of Lipari?

If these are freedom's messengers,
What is their word to Italy?
What hope for island prisoners,
What follows after victory?
Will men who turned their coats in time
Into the seats of power climb,
Or prisoners of Lipari?

The great armada of the air
Brings captive nations liberty,
But what of those in dungeons there,
Who fought the common enemy,
And lost the fight? with aching eyes,
Like shipwrecked men they watch the skies,
They watch the skies, on Lipari.

## WOMAN POWER

*[After Sir Walter Scott]*

O woman in the days of peace,
Mere toy of masculine caprice,
A drug upon the labour mart,
Not called upon to play thy part,
In war, so far as men allow,
A positive sheet-anchor thou!
To-day, in Britain's finest hour,
Thou art described as woman-power.
Thou hast acquired mechanic skill,
The ranks of absent men to fill;
But in the day of victory, when
Thou art superfluous again,

Thy wartime place thou must vacate
In the best interests of the State,
Admitting with submissive grace
That home is Woman's chosen place.


## PLAYING BALL

General Badoglio is playing ball with the Allies. — Reuter. *Evening
News.*

It was raspberries, raspberries all the way,
When Badoglio joined in the game of ball;
You can trust a general for good clean play,
But the patriots' hopes begin to fall —
If the Allies pardon who will repay?

Ex-enemy players, tried and true,
Victor, Roatta, Badoglio,
They come and are welcome — but not a few
Who never played with the common foe
Ask, Why not Keitel and Göring too?

Pillars and props of the old régime,
Does their present aid make a future claim?
What then? Need the Allies be too extreme?
If the Captain's willing to play the game
It's an awkward matter to shoot the team.

The ball game calls for a sportsman's truce,
If those who play by the rules abide;
Timely turncoats may have their use;
If they turn in time to the winning side
They need not stew in the Fascist juice.

And what can the people ask for more?
Would they fight it out to the bitter end
If the victors are ready to wipe the score
By playing ball with a Fascist friend?
Bravo, Badoglio! *vive le sport!*

## CROWN JEWELS

What gives this little isle its high Imperial style,
What makes us heir to ancient Rome's renown?
It's the Crown administration of a native population,
Of the black man, and the yellow and the brown.
What keeps us on the top is our last Imperial prop,
The harvest of historical aggressions —
The subject lands outspread where the map is coloured red,
Our exclusively colonial possessions.

The League-mandated powers do not make the Mandates ours,
Excepting in Imperial opinion,
Nor has Great Britain's word any chance of being heard
In the Commonwealth self-governing Dominion.
The backward folk alone can be reckoned as our own,
Justifying Oriental ceremonial;
We are one among the rest as a nation of the west,
But first among the Powers called colonial.

The Charter does not run in the lands by Britain won
(And exploited by the old Imperial school)
But we ourselves will hand to every subject land
Their Charter of colonial home rule,
Till every native child in the tropic southern wild
Receives the Briton's birthright as a gift —
Till the brown man and the black get their independence back,
In the hope they will not choose to cut adrift.

If we would not fade at last like the Empires of the past,
And be gathered into death without a dawn,
And bewail our vanished might as a Soviet satellite
Or a transatlantic economic pawn;
If we wish to pull our weight as a ruling Empire State
With ascendancy material and moral,
As our sovereignty wanes we must salvage what remains —
Our tropic belts and far-flung reefs of coral.

Our empire in the end on the black man must depend,
And the love of lesser breeds we have to earn,
For to win black men's consent to Imperial government
Is every living Englishman's concern.
Britons now must welcome in citizens of darker skin
Not cold-shoulder fellow subjects of the Crown,
We can ill-afford to chill colonial goodwill
By browning off the black men and the brown.

# CONTINENTAL CHARTER

Full agreement reached in Moscow Three-Power Talks. *Press Headlines.* October 30th, 1943.

The Charter of the Continent
Which Moscow delegates present
Creates an all-time precedent
In lightning accord;
The Conference, convened in haste,
Although with thorny questions faced,
Through its involved agenda raced
While Moscow salvoes roared.

The envoys to their tasks applied
With energy intensified,
As Soviet armies like the tide
Drew near the Dnieper Bend;
At each spectacular break-through
The Three-Power spokesmen closer drew,
And routine business fairly flew
To reach a whirlwind end.

The Talks sped on without a check,
The experts galloped neck to neck —
Not Casablanca nor Quebec
Showed Allies more agreed;
And though some matters had to drop
(Which might have brought them to a stop)
From Kremenchug to Perekop
They never slackened speed.

And when agreement was complete
(A striking diplomatic feat)
With broken Panzers in retreat
Back in confusion hurled,
Loud salvoes from the global Press
(Which had expected rather less)
Announced the Moscow Talks' success —
Twelve days that shook the world.

The enemy's decisive rout
Dissolved all trace of lingering doubt,
All knotty points were straightened out
In three-part unison.
Each day fresh triumphs in the field
New reasons for accord revealed,
Until the Pact was signed and sealed
That steppe by steppe was won.

# FESTUNG LONDON

The main Moscow reaction can be summarized 'Increased danger of peace. Business was discouraged'. — Daily Paper City Notes, November 3rd.

The world sends Moscow greeting,
The Moscow salvoes boom,
The Hitler hordes retreating
Proclaim the Nazis' doom.
The spokesmen of all States enthuse,
And only in the City news
Misgiving and alarm diffuse
Despondency and gloom.

Gilt-edged no longer glitters,
War Stocks trace downward curves,
While sympathetic jitters
Show Wall Street's state of nerves;
The markets have a selling bout,
Lest peace should suddenly break out,
As Hitler, to arrest the rout,
Throws in his last reserves.

Stockbrokers read the headline,
Investors scan the maps.
Will Stalin beat the deadline?
Can Mannstein close the gaps?
At every Eastern Front break-through,
Morale goes down a point or two;
News that the Western Front is due
Brings on a fresh relapse.

When Eisenhower dallied
With Italy's old clique,
The markets rose, and rallied
When Smuts began to speak;
But with the Moscow Conference
The situation grew more tense,
They registered lost confidence
And closed extremely weak.

Three-Power collaboration
Has rung the Third Reich's knell,
And wartime speculation
Has had a knock as well.
As Nazis face catastrophe,
Alarm and black despondency,
A wave of peace psychology
Hits London's citadel.


## JAQUES ON BEVERIDGE

All the world's a workhouse,
And men and women mostly merely paupers,
Liable to accident and unemployment,
Industrial disease and disability,
And doomed from year to year to rot and rot.
But under State Insurance for Security,
Contributory or non-contributory,
Behold the poor from extreme want relieved
Throughout their seven ages.  First the infant,
Mewling and puking of pre-natal benefit,

(Assessed for the unborn at eighteen shillings,
The baby's fifty-fifty split with Ma),
And then the schoolboy, started with eight bob,
Creeping like snail towards school-leaving age
With fifteen shillings training maintenance;
And next the stripling, with one pound a week,
Passing through courtship to the marriage dowry,
A statutory tenner; then the husband,
Protected by the housewife's policy,
And pension (joint) of forty shillings (basic)
Plus extra unemployment compensation.
And then the father,
With multiplying family allowances
(Eight shillings for each pair of pattering feet)
His dwelling crammed with under-age dependants,
And so he earns his meed.  The next age shifts
To the progressive old-age-pensioner,
With fourteen silver shillings in his poke,
Rising in twenty years to five-and-twenty —
His lifetime's aches doctored by State physicians,
Both domiciliary and institutional,
Who sullenly dispense his medicine.
And so he earns the final gift of all,
Saved by the universal funeral grant
From life's last accident, a pauper's grave,
Sans shroud, sans bier, sans hearse, sans everything.

# A SENSE OF THE PAST

Honourable Members, it would appear, prefer, of deliberate choice, to go back to their Victorian building, with its cramped accommodation and a hundred inconveniences ... dominated by the spirit of Gladstone and Disraeli. — *Spectator*, November 5th.

The House! what memories cluster
Around that vanished fane!
Though elsewhere Members muster
What tender ties remain!
That homely yet heroic style
Befits the Commons' shrine
And passion for their Gothic pile
Transcends the Party line.

Unanimous nostalgia
The bombed-out Members share;
All suffered from neuralgia
In that fog-filtered air!
What troubles of the throat and nose
They all enjoyed of old!
And every Session ere they rose
They caught the Commons' cold.

Perpetually muffled
In currents dry and warm,
How comradely they snuffled
Through Budgets and Reform!
What though the ventilation was
A menace to hygiene
And generated poison gas
Behind the purdah screen,

That atmosphere baronial,
That traceried decor,
That antique ceremonial
All, all they will restore —
That sense of crowd, that lack of room,
That decorous hubbub,
That storied Chamber steeped in gloom,
Half chapel and half club!

Bleak winds of reconstruction
May elsewhere freely range,
That cosy reproduction,
Ah! who would wish to change?
Away with harsh modernity,
Hard, chaste, severe and cold!
The renovated House will be
Exactly like the old.


# TEHERAN

The beauty of the surroundings, the secrecy and the romance appealed to the imagination of everybody there — even the native porters of the Legation appeared to be going around in a warm glow — and must have affected the Big Three. — *Daily Express*, December 7th.

Attend! For Allied Leaders meet once more,
Three Fighting Friends at one in Peace and War.
Here's news by Britain yesterday released,
Which Moscow had revealed the day before.

Descending from an air-borne Caravan
Upon the snow-cooled suburbs of Tehran,
Elected Leaders of the East and West
Convivially confirmed their Master Plan.

There the Big Three reshaped the World entire
According to the democrats' desire,
But of the When and Where and Why and How,
Seek not too diligently to enquire.

Enough to know where Standard Roses swoon,
Beneath a brighter Anglo-Persian moon,
Reclined on carpets which the Shah had spread,
They meet To-day to shape To-morrow's boon.

The timing of their liberating blows
Not Cypresses nor Willows will disclose.
Lo! The Tehran communique remains
As uncommunicative as the Rose.

Enough to know they drained the Brimming Bowl
And in the Wine-cup pledged the shining Goal,
And there, not unprovided with the Grape,
Each Leader was the Party's life and soul.

It sometimes seems that never goes so fast
The Conference as where the Jug is passed,
And consecrated in the living Vine,
Each Toast is more eternal than the last.

Enough to know they sealed their lifelong Vow
With Ruby Vintage underneath the bough,
And in their Cups the Master Knot untied —
Ah! Let this be Intelligence enow.

# FESTIVE FOOD FLASH

Now Christmas is near, raising hopes of good cheer,
As the fruits of our conquests are seen,
And Britons all guess how strategic success
Will enliven the Christmas *cuisine*.

Thus Italy's fall should yield lemons for all,
As Badoglio's goodwill contribution,
For the land of the wops grows superlative crops
And lemons lie round in profusion.

Then England awaits some Fighting French dates,
Expected before Christmas Day,
And wine from Algiers is a prospect that cheers,
If it does not turn sour on the way.

Nor should we go short of Doc. Salazar's port,
Now happily bound for our shores,
While the bases he lent us should surely present us
With oranges of the Azores.

The Yankees may send augmented lease-lend,
(For our spam comes in rather thin slices)
Though plum-pudding and pie will be in short supply
While Japan holds the islands of spices.

Our cordial discussions exchanged with the Russians
Should secure caviare for the few;
While all households will share our austerity fare
Of nourishing National stew.

Diplomacy's prize should increase our supplies
No less than the booty of war,
So that all can make merry on sound Franco sherry,
Bought, bonded and bottled by Hoare.

While we are not ungrateful for this hoped-for plateful,
Roast bird is what Britons prefer —
But we note with regret there is no sign as yet
That we will get Turkey this year.


## GLAD TIDINGS

Commercial life will remain in danger for some years, and from commercial danger follows the danger to all those hopes of a better world that depends upon the solvency of our national finances. — Lord Woolton, December 8th.

'God help you, hopeful common men,
Let none be led astray,
On programmes for a better world
There is but this to say,
For signs and wonders do not look,
Bad times are on the way:

O, news of discomfort and care,
Shortage and care,
O, news of discomfort and care!

'We cannot save our shrinking trade
Or make employment sure
Until our business chiefs produce
An economic cure;
In reputation we are rich,
In wealth we shall be poor.

'Much more is our internal debt,
Our income is much less
From gold invested overseas
Which did these islands bless.
Let no one hope for miracles
Or ask for promises.'

So spake unto the common men
The herald Minister
With warnings of lean days to come
For many and many a year,
They all would be with victory
Less well-off than they were.

And as they hearkened to his voice
They mused upon his fame,
And how his plan of rationing
War-shortage overcame,
By pooling all material foods
And sharing out the same.

And from his Yuletide speech they guessed
That hope must not abound,
But be doled out to common men
Like foodstuffs by the pound.
But if they try to ration hope
It never will go round.

O, news of discomfort and care,
Shortage and care,
O, news of discomfort and care!

# FROM THE HORSE'S MOUTH

We'll win the European war in 1944. — General Eisenhower,
December 27th.

Which is the year to be signed with our victory?
Experts predict and commanders confer;
Well-informed comment is still contradictory —
This is the year.

Loud is the conflict of diverse opinions,
Caution marks Whitehall's and Washington's views,
Warnings are heard from the far-flung Dominions —
This is the news.

Roosevelt will venture on no undertaking,
Churchill still warns us of two years to wait,
Hull cannot guess when the clouds may be breaking —
This is a date.

This is the year when the Fortress will fold up,
This is the year when the New Order quits,
This is the year when the map will be rolled up,
This is *the* blitz.

This is the year when the Wehrmacht surrenders,
This is the year when they give up the fight,
For the Third Reich, encircled, and all its defenders,
This is good night.

Over all voices this voice has priority,
No power on earth will our knock-out deter,
We have it this year on the highest authority,
This is the year.

# FOREIGN OFFICE MUSING

A pro-Allied *coup d'état* in Bulgaria is reported from Berne, says the *New York Times.* — *Evening Standard*, January 4th.

A news-flash to-day is reported
From Sofia, through New York and Berne,
A rumour (no doubt much distorted)
That Bulgaria is just on the turn.
Though evidence so far is scanty
It would be to the Office a blow,
If the Government, formerly 'anti',
Should now become 'pro'.

The news, still without confirmation,
Would be most unwelcome, if true,
Of such a transformed situation
We hold a disparaging view.
Sofia's régime, though unstable,
Was not meant, as yet, to be changed,
And the whole Foreign Office time-table
Would thus be deranged.

It would be little short of disaster
If revolt of a popular type
Made Commanders in Cairo move faster,
Before dispositions were ripe.
Political warfare's direction
New angles would have to discuss;
The unspeakable Bulgar's protection
Devolving on us.

The demands of Algiers and Apulia
Have stretched all our trained personnel,
And their functions precise and peculiar,
Would cover to Sofia as well.
We would have to arrange occupation
On quite unfamiliar ground,
And currency notes (for inflation)
Would have to be found.

Bulgarian-speaking officials
Would be called for the Old Guard's support —
An AMGOT (with censored initials)
And initials are now running short.
The Axis should plainly relieve us
And keep Balkan order and law —
To burdens already most grievous,
This adds the last straw.

In propping ex-enemy Powers
We find that the going is rough,
And our satellite windfalls, in showers,
Already are more than enough.
We deprecate any idea
Of Bulgaria changing its side,
And we trust the bad news from Sofia
Will soon be denied.

# WHITED SEPULCHRE

Mr. Roosevelt does not favour Geneva as the seat of a future League because of the aura of failure overhanging that city. — Reported interview with the President of the U.S.

The sepulchre was whited, its outside fair and clean,
But everything within those walls was morally obscene.
And round the mausoleum clings a kind of charnel smell,
No whitewash can eliminate nor time itself dispel.

To sessions at Geneva the Nations came in crowds —
Great Powers wore off-white surplices, weak Members donned
    their shrouds;
Some gathered there to be betrayed and others to betray,
And all without was righteousness and all within decay.

When accusations reached their ears from immolated lands
The Council called for water, the Assembly washed its hands —
Greece, Vilna, Abyssinia, Manchukuo, Spain, Corfu,
These will not be forgiven them for what they did they knew.

And when from Europe's ashes the nations rise once more
To frame another Covenant to stop another War,
Wherever on the Continent this Phoenix-League may light,
It must avoid for evermore that inauspicious site,

And in Geneva's Palace lay that execrated wraith
With all its sanctimonious fraud and tale of broken faith;
Though pious resurrectionists would roll away the stones,
It is a whited sepulchre and full of dead men's bones.

# HOAREY STORY

Franco is a fascist,
Franco is a cheat,
Spain has put a time-bomb
Under Franco's seat;
Franco fights the people,
Franco beats the Crown,
Franco trusts to Britain
Not to let him down.

Neutral, fascist Franco
On Britain's aid depends —
Franco is ungrateful
To faithful British friends.
Spaniards in the *Wehrmacht*,
Nazis in Tangier —
Britain sends a protest,
Franco doesn't hear.

British friends of Franco
Trust his Royal Duke —
Whitehall sends a protest,
Franco cocks a snook.
While the aid of Britain
Tightens Franco's clutch
Some may think that Britain
Doth protest too much.

Franco backs the Axis,
We express regret,
Eden sends a warning,
(Alba bears the threat).
Franco puts his time-bombs
On a British ship . . .
Foreign Office protests
Are Franco's comic strip.

75

No damned flies on Franco,
No damned flies on Hoare,
Protests and offences
They mutually ignore.
Franco's doing nicely
Spanish hopes are sunk
While the British lion
Protects the fascist——Excellentisimo Señor de
   Francisco Franco, Jéfe del Estado, Generalisimo
   de los Ejércitos.


## CO-BELLIGERENT?

The halt in our march upon Rome
Too easily daunts and dismays us,
As War Office spokesmen at home
Set out to explain what delays us;
The Appian Way is no distance,
If we're not yet securely astride,
And we know, if in need of assistance,
Badoglio fights on our side.

His ex-Fascist troops we employ,
Renowned for their deathless audacity,
And resolved for the House of Savoy
To die with the utmost tenacity.
Their gallantry, dash and endurance
Add strength to the forces Allied,
We slog on with the heartening assurance
Badoglio fights on our side.

Though the battle has gone rather worse
Since Badoglio stood Rome's defender,
And our armies have met with reverse
Ever since the Italian surrender,
Our High Command's high expectation
Has been in the main justified —
As we struggle for Rome's liberation,
Badoglio fights on our side.

Palermo we took on our own;
We took Naples in spite of the weather;
We drove on from Salerno alone,
But at Anzio we're sticking together.
The climate throughout has been rotten,
And setbacks cannot be denied,
But now, it must not be forgotten,
Badoglio fights on our side.

The Marshal's belligerent aid
Has given such full satisfaction
That interest has not been displayed
In the sphere of political action;
But while our strategic intention
Must everything else override,
It ought to be worthy of mention
*That Italy is on our side.*

# WELLS OF ARABY

You will remember that the Atlantic Charter touched upon the question of equal access to raw materials in the post-war world. — Robert Waithman in article on 'American Oil in the Middle East', *News Chronicle*, February 18th.

We have no territorial ambition,
We fight to bring an evil to an end,
We fight to raise the common man's condition,
We stand as fighting friend with fighting friend,
We do not bargain for post-war position
Partaking of the love-feast of lease-lend;
No land we covet and no State despoil,
But we must have our share-out of the oil.

The issue of the war is now decided,
Though grim and testing trials lie in wait,
And mankind's destiny, to us confided,
Will be blue-printed at some future date,
But how supplies of oil shall be divided,
On this we do not dare procrastinate,
Nor can we relegate to other hands
Our interests in oil-bearing lands.

We have hurled back the forces of aggression
We have set free Arabia's open spaces,
And by no weight of arms, but by concession
We peacefully exploit the oil bases,
Confirmed in overlordship and possession
By Arab kinglets in their calm oases,
As Power presiding in the Middle East,
Where palms rise up, and every palm is greased.

Our prior claim is due to the exertion
Of our Imperial vision and foresight,
Protected by our mandate Anglo-Persian,
The Shah of Persia wields his sovereign might,
Therefore we question Ibn Saud's conversion
Into a Standard Oil satellite,
While State Department oil is poured upon
The troubled waters of the Lebanon.

Agreed on ideological abstractions
Reiterated at each Conference,
We cannot lightly pass encircling actions
In our established zones of influence,
Nor can our bonds, in Allied oil transactions,
Affect our bargaining and business sense,
Joint victory our friendship will not cool —
Our hearts are one; our oil we cannot pool.

# CHANSON INÖNÜ

## [After Ernest Dowson]

Last night, ah, yesternight when Papen came to dine
The shadow of the Big Three seemed to spread
Athwart the feast between the *Sauerkraut* and the wine;
But though he wooed me with Teutonic passion,
And though through Cairo Nights I kept my head,
I have been faithful to the Allies in my fashion.

Long, long I have directed the Ballet Ankara,
My star attractions both sides strove to please;
At Cairo and Adana they praised my repertoire,
And though impervious to belligerent passion,
Through all sweet seductions of strip-tease
I have been faithful to the Allies in my fashion.

I have danced 'Façade', I have danced 'Rendezvous',
I have danced varieties of the pirouette,
I have repeated 'Les Divertissements Inönü',
The object of unprecedented passion,
I have been doped with Third Reich drugs — and yet
I have been faithful to the Allies in my fashion.

I have ogled all alike with eyes of the gazelle,
Dancing with many veils before the maddened throng,
But when the Allies rushed me, and my yashmak fell,
They knew me unresponsive to their passion
And said my entertainment was too long.
I have been faithful to the Allies in my fashion.

I cried for bigger contracts and for stronger arms,
When the Big Three were kneeling at my feet —
Surely I must defend my unprotected charms!
But something suddenly has killed their passion.
Yet, though I only dance the 'Turkish Suite'
I have been faithful to the Allies in my fashion.

# SATELLITIS

Certain stars shot madly from their spheres. — *Midsummer Night's Dream.*

The Finnish envoys brought it,
Then Hungary straightway caught it,
Next Bucharest
The plague confessed
Though Axis doctors fought it.
The Ukraine rout began it,
When Red troops overran it,
And overnight
Each satellite
Required a change of planet.

Premonitory fright is
The cause of satellitis,
The patient tells
Of fainting spells
And symptoms of St. Vitus.
The pulses madly quicken,
The victims shake and sicken,
The fever flush,
The panic rush
Proclaim the planet-stricken.

Each satellite pretender
Must soon its place surrender,
They were but bright
With borrowed light
And shed reflected splendour.
With signs of deep depression
They wobble in procession,
But solar laws
Permit no pause
And sanction no digression.

Once round the Axis wheeling,
Now off their orbit reeling,
Afraid to stop
In case they drop,
They have that sinking feeling.
They see with souls prophetic,
Survival hypothetic
As a mightier force
Deflects their course,
A body more magnetic.

The satellitic cases
Unhinged in solar spaces,
As the great Red Star
Dims the swastika,
Aspire to change their places.
Acute disorientation
Afflicts the constellation,
Each asteroid
That leaps the void
Foresees annihilation.


# TRUCE

To Italy now stewing in her juice,
Tripartite Powers extend the Party truce —
No by-elections for the head of State,
Badoglio is the coupon candidate.

# THE CALL

England! Let God arise and smite His foes,
The arm of the Almighty let us borrow!
But enemies of God to-day, God knows,
May be our co-belligerents to-morrow.

# HONOURS EVEN

The Russian object now is quick victory . . . the issue of the war can be decided in the strategic area of southern Poland. The Wehrmacht has been defeated in the Ukraine; it will be defeated in Rumania. — Max Werner, April 9th.

Now the Third Reich is encircled, now doom on the Fortress descends,
Who shall apportion the glory due to the Fighting Friends?
Vile is captious division, odious it is to compare,
We are a band of brothers, and common exertions we share.

Now the last act is approaching; and we know the last act crowns the
    play;
If the Soviet rolls back the invader, we are keeping inflation at bay;
If Stalin upholds our endeavour in the sphere of strategic designs,
Our task is conducting world-conflict on the soundest financial lines.

Britain and Russia together honour their valiant sons,
London with salvoes of savings, Moscow with salvoes of guns!
Mighty the forces in action, but ours, in the making, more vast —
What though they march forth to the climax when the climax already
    is past?

83

Three Powers have shouldered the burdens and all in achievement
 assist,
We have provided the armour for the Soviet to mail the fist,
We stand on the threshold of action, prepared for unlimited loss,
While Red Army divisions sweep forward with only one river to
 cross.

In the West we shall force a decision, we are ready, whatever the price,
Though the Wehrmacht, destroyed on the East Front, may not need a
 hammering twice!
Who singles one Ally for honour, the others of honour would rob —
American lent us the tools, and Russia will finish the job.


## NOT FOR EXPORT

Monarchy may still have a useful and important part to play in the
stabilization and reconstruction of Europe if ... it rediscovers its
essential democratic function, which is fully understood and observed
in this country. — *Observer*, April 18th.

The Englishman's affection for the royal institution
Began when wayward Kings had been discrowned;
Our Monarchy's the product of the Glorious Revolution
And the Sovereign is Constitution-bound.
The Continent, a mass of constitutional confusion
Can never hope to imitate the English Constitution.

The European ruler is not seldom contumacious
Denouncing parliamentary control;
The Sovereign of England has only to be gracious,
Refraining from a more dynamic role;
A Monarchy committed to political exclusion
Is the undisputed essence of the English Constitution.

84

Our Monarch is exposed to democratic adulation,
But the contract on both sides is understood;
The King of England does not hope to rule above his station —
He has but one royal duty — to be good.
His spotlessness in private life fulfils his contribution —
A precedent peculiar to the English Constitution.

If King and Constitution feel a mutual revulsion,
Since Parliament the Throne's pretensions quelled,
There follows but a minor Constitutional convulsion,
In which the tainted wether is expelled,
And abdicating sovereigns never dream of restitution
When once they are ejected by the English Constitution.

Ex-Majesties of England drop ambitions of ascendancy,
No longer they invoke the Right Divine,
Retiring with content to some Colonial Dependency
While Parliament joins up the Royal Line;
But ex-Kings of the Continent plan subsequent intrusion —
They would not stand an earthly with the English Constitution.

The Constitution, not the King, is arbiter of Britain,
Since Kings by leave of Parliament have reigned,
But as the Constitution is entirely unwritten
It follows that it cannot be explained.
To European kingdoms it can offer no solution,
For only England understands the English Constitution.

# BALANCE SHEET

The way in which banks and business concerns have adapted themselves to wartime conditions is remarkable ... For India 1943 was a year of conflicting experiences; practically universal prosperity on the one hand, and a distressing shortage of foodstuffs on the other. — Chairman's Report, National Bank of India.

When we survey the Indian situation
  We must be struck by two conflicting trends,
On the one hand, want, famine and starvation,
    And on the other, soaring dividends;
Which wakes reflections of a fruitful kind
  In the contemplative financial mind.

On the one hand, a record of prosperity
  Unequalled even in the days of peace,
And on the other, symptoms of austerity,
    Resulting all too often in decease.
Due, it is generally understood,
  To shortage of the minimum of food.

On the one hand, the business curve ascending,
  Reflecting boundless credit on us all,
And on the other, lack of power of spending,
    Particularly noticed in Bengal,
Where millions showed decreased initiative
  Combined with inability to live.

Which seems to show the power of adaptation,
  So marked in fields of commerce and of trade,
Was absent in the native population
    Which, rather, passive listlessness displayed —
A non-co-operation with the Raj,
  Which might appear as almost sabotage.

India, when thus objectively inspected,
   Discloses contradictions quite immense —
Two sections, to the selfsame strains subjected,
   Reveal a conflict in experience.
One half the world, we feel with fresh surprise,
   Does not know how the other lives — or dies.


## SEEING IT THROUGH

*[With apologies to A. P. Herbert]*

We hangees on the Underground,
We standees on the bus,
So cheerful on our daily round,
So squashed both out- and home-ward bound,
Why has no Laureate been found
To make a song for us?

How oft bisected in the train,
By pincer doors that slide,
How oft left standing in the rain,
When we had hoped to ride!

How oft exposed to grievous harm
When thrown upon the deck,
How bruised about the leg and arm,
How broken as to neck!

When waiting, at the kerb aligned,
For buses to appear,
How patiently we stand resigned,
How often seem bus drivers blind,
How oft the clippie seems inclined
To turn upon those left behind
A cold, sadistic sneer.

No easy job, or lot, is hers,
But think of her reward!
To wipe poor bloody passengers
From off the running-board.

We hounded, lily-livered mob,
We waiters in the queue,
We also carry on the job,
We also see it through.

We also show the British way,
We think we're simply grand —
So Mr. Citizen, hooray!
Let's give ourselves a hand.


# SNOWDROPS

American military police are popularly known as 'snowdrops'. —
News item.


Snowdrops in the Green Park underneath the hawthorns,
Marching with the Stars and Stripes, drilling on parade,
Giant Yankee snowdrops in the morn of maytime,
Lines of snow-white haloes shining in the shade.
Whiter than magnolia, the crocus or the daisy,
Military snowdrops over six foot tall,
Raised in California, Connecticut and Michigan —
This is something Londoners have never seen at all.

Where the doughboys wander, there the snowdrops follow,
Mobile double snowdrops gliding two by two;
Blossoms of the hawthorn vanish with the springtime,
Army snowdrops flourish all the summer through.
Where the doughboys dally with London's broken blossoms,
Led into temptation through the long strategic lull,
Snowdrop guards remind them of military duty,
Speak to them of Washington, of mother, home and Hull.

Banks of snowdrop sentinels stand at Rainbow Corner,
Regiments are on the spot where thirsty doughboys meet,
Dry for Barclay, Guinness, and Worthington and Watney —
All the public fountains are along the snowdrops' beat.
Where the boys seek hidden springs of Johnnie Walker,
Parched for Booth's or Dewar's at the midnight chime,
Just around the corner they find the snowdrops waiting —
Every bunch is busy when it comes to closing time.

Snowdrops, snowdrops everywhere with snow-white gloves
    and gaiters,
Floral decorations in the pre-invasion scene,
War Department snowdrops with guardian angel faces,
Specially selected to keep the Army clean.
Marching out at sunrise with brass bands playing.
Mopping up the stragglers in the darkest black-out hours,
Whiter than magnolia, the crocus or the daisy,
Crooning to the doughboys in the language of the flowers.

A copy of the *Oxford Concise Dictionary* has been sent to Marshal Tito with the compliments of the Oxford University Press. — *Daily Telegraph*, May 19th.

If Tito relies on the Oxford Concise
And learns the King's English from Fowler,
He will find that his call at the doors of Whitehall
Was a bloomer, a slip, and a howler.
He will learn to correct his unlucky neglect
Of the high diplomatic essentials,
For a Partisan Mission, before recognition,
Can never present its credentials.

The Marshal may know how to tackle the foe,
He may drive back the Wehrmacht with ease,
But he's brought to a halt in his frontal assault
On the War Office *chevaux de frise*.
He may have inferred from the well-chosen word
That Great Britain his effort endorses,
To discover with pain Fowler views with disdain
Auxiliary partisan forces.

The Yugoslavs' share of the arms we can spare
He will learn to describe as a dribble,
The verbal bouquets which cloaks Eden's delays
He will shortly define as a quibble.
As the Marshal reads on he will ponder upon
The old English term *shilly-shally*
And a list keep in mind of the words headed *blind*,
Like blind eye, and blind door, and blind alley.

Acclaimed from a distance for feats of resistance
And applauded for gallant defiance,
He will learn common aims do not constitute claims,
Nor do kind words imply an Alliance.
Though short as before of material of war,
The Marshal will not be insensible
That the *Oxford Concise* for linguistic advice
Is a guide that is quite indispensable.


## NO DOORN?

Lord Vansittart wants to know whether the Government has taken, or will take, steps to ensure that no German criminal shall find asylum in any neutral country. — *Manchester Guardian*, June 29th.


When the beaten Nazi bosses
Have to leave their stolen *schlosses*
Along with their accomplices in crime,
Will they meet with retribution
At the place of execution,
Or contrive a getaway a second time?

Will the chiefs of the New Order,
Safe inside a neutral border
Live in undisturbed possession of their loot,
While their hosts refuse admission
To the writ of extradition
For war criminals the Allies want to shoot?

Will Herr Himmler, if molested,
Find his company requested
By Turkish or Iranian health resorts?
Will von Papen's notoriety
Draw the cream of high society
If he next turns up at Sweden's Winter Sports?

Will the slopes of Grand Canary
Give von Schirach sanctuary?
Will Rosenberg parade at Estoril?
Will we hear of Ley's hegira
To the playground of Madeira
And will Goering show his medals in Seville?

After years of idle guesses
Will we learn that Ruedolf Hess is
In Ankara with Ribbentrop and Co.?
And, by-passing St. Helena,
Will we find that Argentina
Keeps Goebbels as a South American Joe?

Will we hear upon inquiries
Arnim is in Buenos Aires,
When von Neurath and Herr Schacht have signed the peace,
While the principal offender
Is dictating 'Mein Surrender'
At a comfortable chalet in La Suisse?

In spite of Allied ravings
Will they make off with their savings,
And in Istanboul or Teheran find a bourne?
Or upon the next occasion
Will the Allies use persuasion
To make certain that there will not be a Doorn?

# KINDLY WORDS

I have no sympathy with those who think it clever or even funny to insult and abuse the Government of Spain. — Prime Minister May 24th.

> The old Atlantic Charter may intend
> That democratic rights shall be respected,
> But this in time of war, does not extend
> To Spain's last Government, by Spain elected.
> Spain's Government by force was overthrown
> And Spain's Dictator rules by force alone.
>
> The Government of Spain is in suspension,
> Her Parliament its rights does not resign,
> Her tyrant, raised by foreign intervention,
> Rules by no right, elective or divine,
> Franco was by the Axis put in power,
> And backed by Britain in her meanest hour.
>
> The rebel Franco we may recognize,
> He may be kept in his uneasy place,
> But by no argument we may devise
> Can we make out a democratic case.
> He may stand high in Cabinet esteem —
> The Spaniards did not vote for his Régime.
>
> Though approbation on the highest level
> May prove this shabby tyrant suits us well,
> Though from expediency we praise the devil
> And give him leave to run his private hell,
> No 'kindly' word can make legitimate
> This Fascist ruler of the Spanish State.

Franco, the porter of Gibraltar's gates
We may confirm in his dictatorship,
We may pay toll for passage through the Straits,
(The gatekeeper must always have his tip)
We may rejoice in hopes of fruitful trade —
The Spanish people know themselves betrayed.

They know that mankind's Charter has no force,
When, backed by Britain's wartime Cabinet,
Franco is kept upon his evil course;
But Spain remembers, and will not forget
That English lives were also lost in vain
To save the lawful Government of Spain.


## SONG BEFORE SUNRISE
### [*After Algernon Charles Swinburne*]

I call upon all friends of freedom to stand with us now. — General
Eisenhower, June 6th.

France, what of the night?
I watch and I do not sleep,
I hear deep calling to deep,
I under the ocean drowned,
I hear the storm in the height;
My help will come from the sea.
I working underground,
I know I shall rise and be free.

Holland, what of the night?
I watch in the dark and wait
In chains at the fortress gate,
The morning sky will be red.

I hear wings beating in flight,
I may not speak, but I hear;
The waters are over my head
But the end of the night is near.

Norway, what of the night?
I watch by the ocean wall,
I, first enslaved of all.
But my fetters will be undone,
I too shall stand in the fight,
I too, in arms at your side.
The tide is beginning to run
And who shall turn back the tide?

Belgium, what of the night?
I hear but may not reply,
I bleed but I may not cry,
What voice have the slain and the slave?
But my hand is ready to smite,
I see neither sun nor stars;
As one far under the wave
I watch through my prison bars.

Freedom, what of the night?
My tempest will shatter the skies!
The night is ending. Arise!
As billows of ocean beat,
Your pent-up floods in their might
Will burst from their bounds and be free.
The waters are leaping to meet
The thunder and surge of the sea.

# LISTENING POST

President Roosevelt has a plan for a new French Government, with
Albert Lebrun as President. — Report in daily paper.

> America is seated
> At her global listening post,
> Till the Wehrmacht is defeated
> By her liberating host,
> Proclaiming her assistance
> To a people's Government
> And leaders of resistance
> On the far-off Continent.

Her full support is guaranteed to forces democratic,
But she cannot hear them clearly, there is such a lot of static,
The air is such a Babel and the jamming is so strong
That when the leaders' names come through she always gets them
   wrong.

> She is perfectly impartial,
> She respects the people's voice,
> If they vote for King, or Marshal,
> She applauds the nation's choice,
> But when the Allies routed
> The force of Kesselring,
> She thought Italians shouted
> For Badoglio and the King.

She nominated Victor to protect the Constitution,
Badoglio to lead the anti-Fascist revolution,
Then found to her astonishment Italians preferred
Another individual whose name she'd never heard.

> When leaders were selected
> For the ruling of Algiers,
> Her hearing was affected
> By the ringing in the ears;

She banked on French devotion
For Darlan and Giraud,
But after their promotion
She learned they had to go.

She saw the Admiral installed (by popular decision)
And then discovered there had been an error in transmission,
And when this misunderstanding had been finally removed
All Frenchmen hoped her hearing would be very much improved.

Now patriots are calling
From the land of Lafayette,
But reception is appalling
And she cannot hear them yet.
She gives her full attention
To the choice the French proclaim —
She desires no intervention
But she cannot catch the name.

She welcomes freedom's leaders in the order of appearance,
But she suffers from a lot of atmospheric interference.
She cannot catch the words of France; France speaks a foreign tongue,
And when they really say 'de Gaulle', she thinks they cry 'Lebrun'!

# GUNK

A glue has been discovered which will stick anything to anything.
The inventor calls it 'gunk'. — News Item.

They may talk of mankind's federation
As a perfectly practical plan,
They may quote the eight-point Declaration
As the dawn of the new age of man.
They may prate of a world constitution,
But the whole proposition is bunk,
For they have no adhesive solution,
They have not provided the gunk.

The glue that sticks pacts round the edges,
The putty to seal up the joints,
The mortar to plaster the pledges,
The paste that will gum up the points.
They may boost an accord international,
And the Big Four may pose as one chunk,
But the claim is completely irrational
In view of the absence of gunk.

They may hang out humanity's Charter,
They may boost international parity,
And the binding effects of world barter,
And the birdlime of business cum charity.
But their words smack of vain repetition
New pacts, like the old, will be junk,
Because of one vital omission —
The lack of a permanent gunk.

While Powers have nothing to glue them
World pacts are foredoomed from the start,
Though after each war they renew them
They always keep flapping apart.

The framework of world peace is brittle,
And the hopes of mankind will be sunk
While they stick it together with spittle
Instead of producing the gunk.


## THE LAST STRAW

Spanish soldiers of the Blue Division are employed by the Germans
in France to repress the French patriots. — News Item, June 12th.

Our most favoured neutral, the Spanish Caudillo
Has answered the kinds word of Señor Churchillo
By raising divisions of Falangist heroes
To patch up the West Wall as Spain's volunteeros,
Oyé!

Though we were persuaded by Sir Samuello
To spare the Caudillo a spot of our Shell-O,
We never expected armed action would follow.
Spain's new Blue Division is too much to swallow.
Oyé!

Franco is renowned as a good caballero,
And source to the City of much profitero,
But even a neutral whose ways are peculiar
Should not send to war a Brigada Azuliar.
Oyé!

While he fights for Rommello, or even Rundstedto,
We cannot get right with the Red Sovieto;
So in view of this act we most strongly suggesto
That this time Great Britain must send a protesto.
Oyé!

For all the kind deeds of the City and Bank-o
There is no gratitudo in dealing with Franco.
For all the kind words of our Señor Churchillo,
The time has now come to blow up the Caudillo.
Oyé!


# DOWN IN THE FOREST

### [*After Longfellow*]

The International Monetary Conference met at Bretton Woods,
New Hampshire, on July 1st.

When the Great Chief of the White House
Called the tribes of men together
For a Conference on Wampum
In the forest of New Hampshire,
Came the prophets of the nations
Foremost in their craft and wisdom —
Morgenthau, State Secretary
For the Treasury Department
With the Sacred Belt of Wampum;
Keynes, the Treasury Adviser
With his belt of solid sterling,
From the wigwam of Nokomis,
Famed Old Lady of Threadneedle
Street, somewhere in Southern England —
Came the lesser tribal experts,
Came and listened in the forest,
Hearkened to the Big Chiefs' pow-wow
Underneath the fragrant pine trees.

Morgenthau and Keynes together
Wrestled while the others waited,
Smoking, hunting, shooting, fishing,
Waiting to be re-conditioned,
Waiting for a cash-transfusion
From the mighty hoard of Wampum.
Keynes and Morgenthau, the wrestlers,
Fought each point on the agenda.
Keynes urged 'Be not slave to Wampum,
Throw away the truss of Wampum,
Start a Fund for prudent lending,
That all tribes of men may borrow,
Each get credit from the other.
Using anything for Wampum,
Sterling, beads or even fishbones.'
Morgenthau, State Secretary,
Tighter strapped the belt of Wampum,
'My world-bank for reconstruction
Must be on a Wampum basis.'
So they reasoned as they wrestled,
While they both exclaimed together —
'Let us order world finances,
Let us keep away inflation,
Let us stabilize exchanges
For the profit of the people
Bankrupt by the fiery war-trail,
For advantage of the nations,
That the tribes of men may prosper
In the Land of the Hereafter.'

# WHATATURK!

Conversations are afoot in Ankara . . . which may lead to Turkey taking part in the war before the end of the summer. — Associated Press, Ankara, July 12th.

What makes the well-informed assert that peace is now in sight?
It's not the super-spectacle of military might,
It isn't Alexander's threat, or Rokossovky's blow,
Or sweep of Allied victories from Lessay and St. Lo —
It's the absolute conviction of an inner force at work
Which will change the neutral outlook of the perspicacious Turk,
Unenterprising, temporizing, pussyfooting Turk.

The only neutral Ally in the whole united bloc,
Preserved from diplomatic and from military shock,
The Turk, so supersensitive to any hidden snag,
Would never move if victory were not now in the bag,
And when the Turk cuts down on chrome and takes a loss on zinc
It shows that peace is nearer than the Allied generals think.

The forcing of the Niemen, the forward drive from Pinsk,
The great push-off from Plotsk and Pskov, the coming fall of Dvinsk,
Montgomery's advances on the Odon and the Orne,
The Eighth beyond Arezzo and the Fifth beyond Leghorn,
These show the march of victory, but what removes all doubt
Is not the armies pushing on, but Papen pulling out.

Despite official warnings of interminable strife,
New optimistic prophecies are absolutely rife,
As, saved from all contingencies by Allied guarantees,
The Turk is creeping in by imperceptible degrees.
The burdens of full victory this Ally will not shirk,
The ever-wary, every-chary, self-preserving Turk,
The hesitating, calculating, non-committal Turk.

# THE WRITING ON THE WALL

Events inside the Reich seem to show that experienced Generals
have seen the writing on the wall. — Mr. Eden, July 24th.

When all round Europe's Fortress the Allied armies surge,
And Soviet spearheads hammer at the gate,
And Nazi leaders' fancies lightly turn to thoughts of purge
To circumvent the crises in the State,
When the Wehrmacht and the Party stage their first impromptu
   brawl,
The neutrals clearly recognize the writing on the wall.

When now the little rift is seen within the German lute,
Though careless talk inside the Reich is barred,
And all the Home Front Herrenvolk are absolutely mute
With a million S.S. bloodhounds standing guard,
When the Führer screams for vengeance, and Ley and Goebbels
   bawl,
Well, even the civilians see the writing on the wall.

When the Wehrmacht is instructed to adopt the Nazi 'Heil!'
And the *Offizierskorps* has to kiss the rod,
It is perfectly apparent to the Army rank and file
That something in the Reich is wrong and odd.
As the Baltic and the Polish and the Prussian bastions fall,
The Jerries as they run can read the writing on the wall.

When Generals long established on the German General Staff
Win the Order of the Oak Leaves and the Sword,
The honour seems intended as a kind of epitaph,
And is taken as a posthumous award;
There are obsequies attended by the Little Corporal,
For Generals who failed to see the writing on the wall.

When missing Marshals fade away or vaguely disappear
For hindering intuitive designs,
Or meet with fatal accidents while flying to the rear,
Experienced commanders read the signs.
With Himmler standing ready to exterminate them all,
Not even Generals can miss the writing on the wall.


## IF

*[After Kipling]*

If you can hold your tongue when all around you
Will talk about the fly-bombs in their street,
If you've been blasted too, but don't feel bound to
Speak of the bomb that blew you off your seat;
If you could talk about the one that raced you,
And circled, and turned back before it missed,
And how you dashed to shelter as it chased you —
And still have resolution to desist:

If you can be a sympathetic hearer
When others tell you how their glass was blown,
And boast that all their bombs have fallen nearer —
Yet never breathe a word about your own;
If you've seen incidents you do not mention,
Far worse than anything they've seen next door;
If you can give buzz-bomb bores your attention,
And not yourself become a buzz-bomb bore:

If you pursue your daily occupation,
Just as you did before the robots came,
If you can keep them out of conversation
And chat of other matters just the same;

If you've met bombs you never think of sharing,
Though you were right beside them when they dropped,
If you keep mum when others are comparing
What *they* felt like the time the engine stopped:

If you can walk where doodle-trails are blazing,
If you can pass where doodle-gazers gaze,
And you yourself refrain from doodle-gazing,
Though everybody else has caught the craze;
If you can keep aloof from mass suggestion,
If you stand fast while other people flap —
I'll say, my son, without the slightest question,
You must be an extraordinary chap.


# BOMB CONSCIOUS

V2, the new weapon, is something absolutely new. — Berlin Correspondent, *Svenska Dagbladet*, August 13th.

Day bombs, night bombs, late bombs, early bombs,
Buzz bombs, fly bombs, power bombs, whirli-bombs,
Dive bombs, fire bombs and cascade bombs,
Fragmentation and delayed bombs,
Whistlers, screamers, bouncers, jumpers,
Bombs that burst and bombs that hide,
Plungers, dodgers, thudders, crumpers,
Bombs that hover, bombs that glide,
Heavy, medium, large and small,
Londoners have had them all.

High bombs, low bombs, new bombs, old bombs,
Target bombs and uncontrolled bombs,
Fast bombs, slow bombs, lone bombs, blitz bombs,
Wild bombs, trial bombs, oil bombs, sitz-bombs,

Bombs in baskets, bombs in clusters,
Robots, anti-personnel,
Butterfly bombs and blockbusters,
Doodlebugs and hounds of hell,
Every type, no matter what,
Londoners have had the lot.

First of targets and the last,
Scorched with fire and scarred with blast,
London still with London pride
Takes the bombing in her stride,
Though the enemy has sent
Every kind he can invent.
Blitzed, bombarded, but not out,
London now begins to doubt
If the foe can still devise
Any genuine surprise,
Launching missiles from afar
Wholly unfamiliar.
Nazi boasts of Doodle One
Proving greatly overdone,
Have they found in Doodle Two
Something absolutely new?

# BENEDICTION

We have sympathized deeply with your affliction . . . we have prayed
for you daily and hourly . . . we exhort you to bear your trials with
Christian resignation and fortitude . . . and with Christian sentiments
of charity, forgiveness and mercy. — Message from the Pope to
London, August 28th.

> The Vatican with spiritual mien,
> Above the battle's flame and smoke and dust,
> Shines like the universal sun serene
> Alike upon the unjust and the just.
> But seems occasionally somewhat warmer
> When it directs its beams upon the former.
>
> The Papacy in judgment throned on high,
> Arbitrament of earthly war condemns,
> But does not turn the same impartial eye
> Upon the Tiber as upon the Thames —
> Its vision manifests a slight obliquity
> When estimating national iniquity.
>
> It did not Christian charity advise
> And intercede for Greece with constant prayer,
> Nor with the Ethiopians sympathize,
> Nor with the Duce plead his foes to spare,
> Nor for Albanians utter exhortation
> On Christian charity and resignation.
>
> It did not judge war as unrighteousness
> When waged against the followers of Marx,
> Nor Italy's crusade decline to bless
> Against the flock of Greek Church Patriarchs;
> The temporal arm may be the Church's proxy
> Invoked by champions of orthodoxy.

London, that mourns and fights and asks no pity,
Magnificent in ruin, maimed, bereaved,
London, now hailed by the Eternal City,
Replies to Rome, by British arms relieved:
'London might not have suffered this affliction,
Had evil not received Rome's benediction.'


# THE LAST RECESS

Members will spend the Parliamentary recess getting in touch with their constituents. — News Item.

Parliament is in recess.
Trusty Commons on vacation,
After months of storm and stress
May indulge in relaxation,
Spending hours of idleness
At a holiday address.

Do they to the seaside haste,
Paddling on forbidden beaches,
Or the fleeting moments waste
Angling in sequestered reaches?
No; for Members wildly guess
Victory may come express.

Burdened with an uphill task,
Threatened with a new election,
Home the Members flock to ask
Pledges of revived affection.
Nor can they the fear suppress,
This may be their last recess.

Policy is in suspense,
Reconstruction dynamited;
Welcomed once (with reticence),
Beveridge is blitzed and blighted.
Members cannot well profess
Parliamentary success.

Planning's in a fearful state,
Housing in a sad condition,
Controversial matters wait
On the waiting Coalition,
Which, the Members must confess,
Soon may cease to coalesce.

Legislation's in a mess,
Pending further legislation;
Members bringing no redress,
Face constituents' indignation.
Victory may come express,
Parliament is in recess.

## MILESTONE

September 3rd, 1939 – September 3rd, 1944.

However long a war may last
And dates must never be forecast,
The worst is usually past
When five full years have flown;
The first five years are critical
For building war-material
And problems of home-front morale
Must not be left alone.

The first five years must play their part
To give the next five years a start,
To keep war-workers in good heart,
Though every nerve is strained;
War measures must be improvised
And war departments organized,
And everybody mobilized
(Or otherwise detained).

The first five years provide the test
For public cheerfulness and zest,
And keeping up its interest
As belts are tighter drawn;
Therefore the first five years require
Winged words of energy and fire
To waft men's thoughts to something higher —
To wit: the coming dawn.

The first five years of shock endured,
The populace becomes inured,
The end (if not in sight) assured,
Whatever be in store;
Thenceforth war leaders need not fear,
Though victory should not appear
Before the tenth or twentieth year,
Or even somewhat more.

For once the first five years have seen
The gearing of the State machine,
It runs thereafter by routine
With smoothness and success,
No matter if there come to be
(As in some wars of history)
A tinge of creeping apathy
Or slight war-weariness.

And so, with sober confidence,
Begot of vast experience
In wars progressively immense
And globally dispersed,
However lengthy and widespread,
Whatever setbacks loom ahead,
It can be definitely said,
The first five years are worst.

## AMERY'S BRAT

Who was left holding the baby
Cripps laid at the Congress door?
Who'll be left holding the baby
By the end of the Japanese war?

Cripps seemed in a hurry to leave it
In the teeth of the Congress gale;
When India refused to receive it
Her leaders were clapped into gaol.

The Raj is the baby's stepmother,
So Congress will not be its nurse;
No Hindu will call it a brother,
It has the Mohammedan's curse.

They passed it to Gandhi to save it,
Though the baby was Amery's brat,
Then Gandhi asked Jinnah to have it,
But Jinnah just turned it down flat.

All parties in India disown it,
It is subject to constant attack,
Now Gandhi to Wavell has thrown it,
And Wavell has hurled it right back.

The infant has always been ailing,
Its hope of survival is small;
Each day it is visibly failing,
It has no Constitution at all.

This is the Government baby
Which India declines to adopt.
If no one's left holding the baby,
The baby is bound to be dropped.

## DON'T LET'S BE BEASTLY TO AMERICA

If America seems lately
To be burning for a row,
It doesn't matter greatly,
For she's not herself just now.
Her condition is affecting,
For she's just come over queer —
Yes, America's expecting,
And her time is drawing near.

If she sees her spangled banner
Waving everywhere alone,
We must keep the bedside manner
And refuse to flaunt our own.
If she feels pre-natal craving
For the fruits of all the earth
We must still indulge her raving,
Till America gives birth.

If she seems perverse and fretful,
To the British Commonwealth
We must never be forgetful
Of her present state of health;

Like the eagle when she's broody,
Like the lioness with whelp,
If America is moody
It's a thing she cannot help.

If she wants to start the rumour
That the British never fought,
We must cherish her, and humour,
For we know she is distraught;
We must still contrive to love her
While she bares her claws and fangs;
For these demonstrations cover
Her preliminary pangs.

We must not attempt to change her,
Nor her indignation rouse,
Till the Dewey little stranger
Has arrived at the White House,
Or till Roosevelt on election
Celebrates victorious morn —
She'll return our tried affection
Once a President is born.


## NO OTHER POLES

A crisis is commonly critical
    For a week, or a day, or an hour,
If simply and solely political
    It ends with a transfer of power.
It may ease with a change of authority
    Or respond to external controls,
A vote may assert the majority —
    But not with the Poles.

The crisis of Poland is static,
    It always remains at the peak,
It defies the approach diplomatic
    Which works with the Finn and the Greek.
The Balkans may reach a solution
    With rulers reshuffled in shoals,
They may patch up a new Constitution —
    But never the Poles.

Some nations reveal schizophrenia,
    Ex-Fascists from Fascists divide,
We hear of 'the other Rumania'
    'Good' Italy fights on our side.
There are 'bad,' there are 'better' Bulgarians,
    'Good' Finns may come out of their holes,
There's a choice between Reds and Agrarians
    There are no 'other' Poles.

The crisis is Poland's tradition,
    Like Poland, Poles never give in,
Poles holding the London position
    Are Polish as those in Lublin.
The Poles will not brook interference,
    Diehards to the depths of their souls,
So their crisis has every appearance
    Of lasting as long as the Poles.

# DUMBARTON HOAX

*[After Lewis Carroll]*

They sent us word that they had met
And told us not to tell;
Until the programme was upset
It went extremely well.

The three involved in the affair
Talked very fast indeed,
And did their best to clear the air
Before they disagreed.

They told us matters were improved
And useful ground was gained,
But when the deadlock was removed
The *impasse* still remained.

One mentioned that he could not say
What three should try to do,
But then it seems the trouble lay
Between the other two

We gave them two, they gave us one,
And that is all we got,
Though both agreed what should be done
If one did you-know-what.

We said two must do this and that
If one did thus and thus,
They parleyed for a future chat
Between themselves and us.

Since one and two have failed to win
The full assent of three
The whole affair has ended in
A blaze of secrecy.

# WAR OFFICE BABY

*[After George Macdonald]*

A Middle East general order has announced that married Service men
could obtain compassionate leave to start a family. — News Item.

Where did you come from, baby dear?
Out of the Middle East into here.

How did you fly through the pearly gate?
My Mum had a doctor's certificate.

Why did you not come here before, sweet tot?
I don't quite know, but I guess a lot.

Where did you get those wondering eyes?
My Dad's return was a great surprise.

And where did you get that expression naive?
It's something to do with compassionate leave.

Whence comes, baby darling, that smile of bliss?
The colonel blew me a birthday kiss.

And why did they want you, pretty pet?
The War Office hasn't informed me yet.

And how did you get here, little lad?
The Army said it was up to Dad.

Whence came dimpled fingers and toes, sweetheart?
The Army said Dad must make a start.

What makes you so rosy from feet to head?
That's what King's Regulations said.

Whence that gold hair like an angel's harp?
H.Q. said Mummy had best look sharp.

How did all this come to be you, sweet lamb?
My Daddy was posted and here I am.

Where does the War Office come in, my dear?
Grigg thought about babies, so I am here.


## CROSSING THE FLOOR

*[Respectfully dedicated to Rt. Hon. C. Attlee]*

The National Executive desire that when the time comes to dissolve what has been a great partnership, the dissolution should be accomplished with dignity and good feeling. — Labour Party National Executive statement, October 7th.

Daybreak and morning light,
    And one clear Party cleft!
And may there be no carping at the Right
    When I lead out the Left

The harbour almost gained, the voyage done,
    The best of messmates soon must say farewell;
The time cannot be far when for each one
    Tolls the division bell.

Beyond the bar the shoals and sandbanks shift,
    The crew can scarcely keep the craft afloat —
Bound for uncharted seas I cast adrift,
    And seek the vote.

When I alone the ship of State may guide,
　　Still with one backward look I'll change my place —
No longer with my Captain side by side,
　　But face to face.

My trusty shipmates I shall keep in mind,
　　While tacking to the Opposition shore —
And may there be no sniping from behind,
　　When I have crossed the floor.


## FOR FREEDOM

Italian prisoners of war billeted in houses in Pinner are to be removed,
following strong public protests.

Hail! liberated Athens,
　　Relieved by patriot bands,
The symbol of resistance
　　In subjugated lands.
Hail, champions of freedom
　　Who still their homes defend,
And hail! victorious Pinner,
　　And glorious Hatch End!

Against the homes of Pinner
　　The War Department came,
But Pinner breathed defiance
　　And Hatch End burst in flame.
When Pinner struck for freedom,
　　When Hatch End stood for right,
The War Office was worsted,
　　For all its armoured might.

From Harrow down to Watford
  The news of battle flies,
In Middlesex they rally
  And Bucks begins to rise,
The patriots of Chiswick
  Give battle street by street,
The partisans of Ealing
  Have forced a mass retreat.

On every hearth in Pinner
  They feed the sacred fire,
The War Department tyrants
  Like beaten curs retire.
Hail! liberated Athens
  Which stands for freedom still!
And hail! victorious Pinner
  By Harrow on the Hill.

## POT-LUCK AT THE KREMLIN

Mr. Churchill has once more in the interests of the Grand Alliance
exposed himself to the dangers of an autumnal journey and the ardours
of Muscovite hospitality. — *Observer*, October 22nd.

When statesmen fly to a vital meeting
For the global weal of the human race,
State hospitality follows greeting
And ceremonial feasts take place.
A banquet cannot be flashed by cable,
The bonds that last must be forged at table —
The statesman's task is the task of eating,
When friend with fighting friend keeps pace.

The White House feast is a small collation
With scalloped lobster and clam broth clear,
Where chicken *créole* aids conversation,
And planked shad lightens the task severe,
Where strawberry shortcake and gorgeous ices
Sweeten the statesmen's sacrifices.
But greater ardours of mastication
Await in the Eastern Hemisphere.

There are strains and stresses gastronomic,
Endured for the welfare of all mankind,
When the guest is served by the host Slavonic,
And the White House *cuisine* is left behind.
There are stricter tests, there are sterner ardours
When the feast wells forth from the Kremlin larders,
And the burden of banqueting seems more chronic,
When none of the dishes may be declined.

There are Chlodniks, Kabobs and Stschi to swallow,
Sturgeon fresh from the Caspian coast,
Bortsch and truffles and carp to follow,
And Russian bitocks, the Kremlin's boast.
The valiant visiting stomachs wrestle
With oyster and caviare, Moscow Special,
Till the void is filled and the dish is hollow,
And each course crowned with a comrade's toast.

And hope for the future is visibly brightened
As statesmen strive in the Kremlin hall,
The cloud of suspicion (if any) is lightened,
And problems into perspective fall.
The bonds of friendship are forged and tested,
The indigestible is digested,
And belts are loosened, but ties are tightened
When statesmen dine for the good of all.

# O, FOR THE WINGS OF A DOVE!

O, for the wings, for the wings of a dove,
To fly to a lone destination,
When peace brings the era of brotherly love,
And the dogfights for peace aviation!
The Big Business racket, the plan to attack it,
Disrupt the united Allies:
Air traffic commercial becomes controversial
And cormorants cover the skies.

When warplanes were pooled for strategical flights
Men hoped the arrangement was permanent,
But now private enterprise fights for its rights
To tie up and dole out the firmament.
Should traffic be rationed? Is trade-war old-fashioned?
Who may ply for the profits of peace?
Is it free competition or world-wide submission
To a force of aerial police?

As seafaring Powers once fought for their share
In command of the great ocean highways,
Now Powers contest territorial air,
And the battle is joined for the skyways.
The place on the rota, the size of the quota,
Are matters of careful research,
If law must take over from the lawless air-rover
And issue permission to perch.

The Big Four who sang as a tuneful quartet
At all world-events they attended,
Have now been reduced to a straggling duet
With voices imperfectly blended.
The Civil Air Meeting with two plans competing,
Provokes acrimonious words
On co-operation for air mass-migration,
So easily managed by birds.

# ROYAL INTERNATIONAL

The Pope gave an audience to Ex-Crown Prince Rupprecht of Bavaria last Thursday. Austrian Catholic leaders in Rome are known to favour a Catholic Federation of Austria, Bavaria and perhaps part of the Rhineland after the war. — *La Suisse*, November 4th.

Rupprecht von Wittelsbach calls on the Pope,
    Otto von Habsburg has cropped up,
Royalist circles see vistas of hope
    When Europe's Republics are mopped up.
Habsburgs are Holy as well as Imperial,
Their annals are old and their story is serial.

Family thrones they are ready to fill,
    As Presidents fall with their Ministries,
From Chile, Bolivia, Peru and Brazil
    Flock claimants of dead and gone dynasties.
With papal support (and a thumping majority)
Pretenders receive a high travel priority.

Wettins may sit upon Saxony's throne,
    Zähringens flourish in Baden,
Württemberg-Brandenburgs get back their own,
    When the tenant vacates Berchtesgaden.
The Third Reich is marked by exceptional brevity,
Habsburgs rejoice in amazing longevity.

Monarchs may rise in the wake of the peace,
    Wittelsbachs reign in Bavaria,
Sonderburg-Glücksburg find welcome in Greece,
    Saxe-Coburgs inherit Bulgaria.
The Vatican offers a new opportunity
For public devotion and Catholic unity.

Ex-Bourbon-Habsburgs in Spain may be found,
    To match Lisbon's Habsburg-Braganza,
Habsburg-Leczinskis in Poland be crowned,
    (They've got a hope or *Esperanza*!)
Catholic courts of antique consanguinity,
Rulers restoring the right of divinity.

Habsburgs and Bourbons safe back in the fold,
    Not to mention the reigning Sardinians,
Wettins and Wittelsbachs throned as of old,
    In sovereign ducal dominions.
Princes and potentates east of the Rhine again!
Ex-Hohenzollerns are getting in line again!
Dukes of Saxe-Coburg, Saxe-Weimar, Saxe-Meiningen!
Royalist circles begin to feel fine again.

## INVISIBLE EXPORTS

When Foreign Office culture sweeps from China to Peru
And the Treasury finances British art,
    Official recognition
    Of the British Council's mission
Proves that culture plays a propagandist part.

The British Council's mandate goes forth from Ind to Ind,
Its lectures do inestimable work;
    The Institute Britannic
    Has ousted the Germanic,
With the Portuguese, the Spaniard and the Turk.

The Council is a riot in Peru and Paraguay,
It has introduced glee-singing in Brazil;[1]
    Its famed Madrid Tertulia
    Has prestige quite peculiar,
It makes Argentinians madly Anglophil.

Enlightened British taxpayers should not begrudge the cost
Which the Treasury so joyfully subscribes,
    As artistic propaganda
    Sweeps Addis and Loanda
And culture captures Equatorial tribes.

The Council's Monthly Letter, a Court Circular in brief,
Has cultural events on every page,
    When visitors of title
    Remark that art is vital,
And culture thrives with Royal patronage.

Accounts of Britain's Planning delight the Angolese,
Art lectures in Baghdad are bearing fruit,
    And a bumper circulation
    Shows widespread appreciation
For 'Life Stories of the Onion, and the Newt'.[1]

Our cultural attachés assist our Empire trade
Through political and diplomatic skill,
    For culture thus exported
    Is officially reported
To buy imports of invisible goodwill.

[1] For this and all other statements of fact above,
see *Report of the British Council*, 1943-4.

# HELLAS REBORN

The isles of Greece, the isles of Greece,
  With Crete and the Dodecanese,
Still bleeding under Hitler's peace
  Which law and order guarantees,
The isles of Greece are not yet free,
  But Athens hails her liberty.

The Greeks have fought their Marathon,
  We praise the patriot Hellenes,
But now their fighting days are done,
  The British Army intervenes,
And troops on duty as police
  Maintain the Foreign Office peace.

Where liberating armies drive
  They quell internal discontent,
And here a dynasty revive,
  And there a puppet Government,
But Athens opened wide her doors
  To comrades, not to conquerors.

Is Greece now a mandated land?
  Is Athens but another Rome?
A little Ally out of hand?
  Has Greece not worked her passage home?
Shall Greek Resistance be put down
  To prop the quislings of the Crown?

The Greeks know well for what they fight,
  No foreign force can keep the peace.
And for what end and by what right
  Shall Britain now dictate to Greece?
Immortal Athens, who are we
  To teach Hellenes democracy?

# UP THE GARDEN PATH

## [*After Christina Rossetti*]

We have been led up the garden path to find there is nothing at the
end of it. — Megan Lloyd George, M.P., on Housing.

And will State housing plans go all the way?
　　Yes, to the very end.
And have you reached the target for to-day?
　　No, not to-day, my friend.

But have you nothing yet that you can show,
　　No homes to allocate?
One prototypal Portal bungalow
　　That hides behind the Tate.

Will Portals then arise in tens, or scores?
　　No, Portal huts are now quite obsolete;
The Phoenix from the Portal ashcan soars,
　　And soon will be complete.

But will there be a Phoenix hutch for me,
　　In rebuilt areas of blitz and blight?
The Phoenix will have high priority
　　When we acquire a site.

Are not locations for rehousing planned,
　　For either 'temps' or 'perms'?
Not yet, but all will soon be put in hand
　　When we arrange the terms.

Time will new fabricated types reveal,
　　Yea, homes for everyone,
Of concrete or asbestos or pressed steel,
　　When once we have begun.

But when will these asbestos huts appear,
  Or steel or tin, or any other kind?
Not yet, but fourteen Ministries, my dear,
  Are keeping them in mind.

This is the garden path; where does it lead?
  I see no roofs, no walls behind the fence,
No dwelling, lean-to, out-house, and indeed,
  Not one convenience.

No hut, no shack, no bungalow, no shed,
  Of steel or brick, of plaster or of lath —
In fact, I've been notoriously led
  Right up the garden path.


## USELESS AND UNACCEPTABLE GIFTS

Now Christmastide comes round once more,
With all its festival *décor*,
The season is appropriate for
Gifts.

Though international good will
And peace are (relatively) nil,
They show the Yuletide spirit still,
Seasonable gifts.

Whitehall a choice of gifts supplies
For Britons, and the small Allies;
Recipients should not scrutinize
Original and useful gifts.

To bring the home front joy and cheer,
White Papers (slightly soiled) appear,
With wishes hopeful and sincere,
Reasonable and inexpensive gifts.

But cheap gift tokens, strange to say,
And bogus Charters on display,
Are even hard to give away
As acceptable or pleasing gifts.

The Poles receive new frontier maps
Where acquisitions balance gaps,
Which Poles do not regard perhaps,
As suitable and appropriate gifts.

The gifts for Greece, unwrapped too soon,
Intended as a royal boon,
Are not considered opportune
Welcome or desirable gifts.

The gifts for Italy designed
Dispatched with greetings firm but kind,
The anti-Fascists do not find
Timely or necessary gifts.

The gifts in Whitehall most admired,
By seasonable thoughts inspired,
Are definitely not desired,
Unattractive, unacceptable, useless, unwelcome,
   inappropriate and utterly superfluous gifts.

# IMAGINARY CONVERSATION

*Scene:* 10 *Downing Street.*

*Characters:* *The Prime Minister: King George of the Hellenes, and his Master of Ceremonies.*

P.M.     Come in, Your Majesty. Pray take a seat.

KING G.  We thank you, we would sooner have our throne.

P.M.     Sooner, you will not.

KING G.                      Later, then? By heaven!
Our Hohenzollern blood begins to boil.
We are the Hellenes' King by right divine,
Yet here we stand, a head without a State,
And there lies Greece, a State without a head:
Both must, and should, and can, and will, be joined.

P.M.     I neither can predict nor guarantee
If, when, or how the royal head shall sit
Crowned on the shoulders of the subject trunk,
But thought it fit we meet and come together,
To state and clarify my policy
Lest I should be misjudged and misconstrued,
Which is, to put it in a word or two,
After resolved and firm conciliation,
With crash of ordnance and with clash of arms,
To leave the whole thing solely to the Greeks.
Our General Scobie leaves it to the Greeks,
Our Mr. Leeper leaves it to the Greeks,
And so the King must leave it to the Greeks.

KING G.  What is this it that we must leave to Greeks?
What is it but ourself? We are the Greeks.
We are the King. You leave the Greeks to us.

P.M.     But if Your Majesty would help your cause,
Then sign this non-committal document
To hasten and facilitate a truce,
When mighty weapons of conciliation
Have curbed and mastered too-tempestuous change.

KING G.   Our abdication we will never sign,
          We are King George and not King Constantine.

P.M.      This is no instrument of abdication,
          But in fulfilment of your Royal pledge
          Not to return before a plebiscite,
          It nominates a Regent for your realm.

KING G.   We will not have our Kingdom held in trust,
          Our subjects ought to trust our kingly word.

P.M.      And so they do, but treasure it so much
          They long to have it down in black and white.

KING G.   We do not trust the Greeks.  If we should sign,
          Will Britain fix the Athens plebiscite?

P.M.      Your Majesty, that is not Britain's way,
          But I have found in my experience,
          Since by my country I was called to bear
          The grievous burdens of democracy,
          A wise majority will vote aright,
          And thus the Right is buoyed and fortified,
          Sustained and nourished by their confidence.
          So it may well be with Your Majesty,
          Although of course I leave it to the Greeks,
          And further, by this present instrument,
          Your prospects will be brightened and improved.
          All may be well.  While Britain holds the ring
          Free Hellenes freely may elect you King.
          Your Majesty may still regain his throne,
          The brightest jewel in the British zone.

(KING GEORGE *signs the document, which his* MASTER OF CEREMONIES *hands
to the* PRIME MINISTER)

# SURPRISE AND REGRET

The publication of King Peter's Statement caused the utmost surprise and regret among British Ministers. — *The Times*, January 12th.

When Balkan bandits disagree
About a Royal Regency,
And inter-Allied harmony
    Is partially upset,
The Ministers assigned to deal
With outbreaks of Resistance zeal,
In diplomatic terms reveal
    Unqualified regret.

But while the Diplomatic Corps
All differences must deplore,
Regret is mixed with something more
    When kings bar compromise.
A breach of Royal etiquette,
Though fortunately seldom met,
Inspires a more profound regret,
    Commingled with surprise.

The Monarch who will not confer
With the appropriate Minister,
Provokes a poignant *cri de coeur*
    From all the Cabinet;
When he rejects what they advise,
His action stuns and stupefies —
Regret is sharpened by surprise,
    Surprise outweighs regret.

The ill-advised communiqué
Spreads Ministerial dismay,
And calls emotions into play
    More hard to analyse —

The Foreign Office stands amazed,
Officials are completely dazed,
Regrets, however suavely phrased,
    Do not conceal surprise.

Despite all past experience,
A lack of Royal confidence
Arouses feelings too intense
    To cover or disguise.
When Kings in exile forget
How deep they are in Britain's debt,
Surprise intensifies regret,
    Regret includes surprise.

## THUNDERER ON THE LEFT

How can we complain of the attitude of hostile newspapers in the United States when we have here in this country witnessed such a melancholy exhibition as that provided by some of our most time-honoured and responsible journals?

Our task has been rendered vastly more difficult by a spirit of gay, reckless and unbridled partisanship which has been let loose on the Greek question. — The Prime Minister in the House of Commons.

Two minds with but one thought of old,
    A case of true affinity,
The Thunderer to men foretold
    The mood of the divinity.
But now the partnership presents
    A cleavage categorical,
The prophet from the God dissents,
    The God rebukes the oracle.

The mighty pillar of the State,
  Above the fight since time began,
Becomes the Devil's advocate,
  The Thunderer's a partisan.
  A gay and reckless partisan,
  Unbridled, feckless partisan,
A touched with Trotsky heterodoxy, harum-scarum partisan.

But has this immemorial guide
  Become a blindfold blunderer?
No, Jove's own bolt is turned aside
  When hurled against the Thunderer.
Outpourings of fanatic heat
  Are nowhere there detectable,
Instead, this grave and reverend sheet
  Makes partisans respectable.

The tempest rolls, the lightnings blaze,
  The contest is Olympian,
The Titans go their separate ways,
  The Thunderer's a partisan.
  A fulminating partisan,
  The culminating partisan,
A still dissentient, independent, unrepentant partisan.


MAD OR SANE?

The Nazis to the Reich explain
Their Führer is both well and sane;
But now his prospects look so bad,
If he is well, he must be mad.

# LUNATIC FRINGE

Remember it is always the lunatic fringe of American comment which is most likely to get cabled to England just because it is the lunatic fringe. — *Manchester Guardian*, January 2nd.

If the lion is piqued
When its tail is tweaked,
And its attitude misrepresented,
We do well to recall
In the interests of all,
That the tweakers are slightly demented.
If the lion with a growl
Plucks America's fowl,
And the eagle complains of a twinge,
This fatuous action
Shows mental distraction —
It's the work of the lunatic fringe.

The voice of ill-will
Is a voice imbecile,
Its charges are frenzied and frantic —
We must not be estranged
By comment deranged
As insults criss-cross the Atlantic.
Inflammable titbits
When published by nitwits
Should not on our friendship impinge.
The drivelling babble
Of the idiot rabble
Belongs to the lunatic fringe.

But the States should explain
Which are bats, which are sane —
Does The Times of New York cause anxiety?
Is the Herald Tribune
From brainstorms immune?
Does the Washington Post need psychiatry?
Is America's Press
All nuts, more or less?
Who is free from a dubious tinge?
Can any be said
To be right in the head?
And which is the lunatic fringe?

The problem is knotty —
Who is sane? Who is dotty?
And where, on this side, are we heading?
Have we newsmen around
Not mentally sound?
Is the fringe of the lunatics spreading?
We confess self-mistrust,
We may all be concussed,
With so much to disturb and unhinge.
O, let us inquire
Before fanning the fire —
Are we part of the lunatic fringe?

In such a home for children of three years, not one of the children
could talk. The matron said: 'They do not need to talk, everything is
done for them.' *Whose Children?* by Lady Allen of Hurtwood.

If they could speak, if we could hear
  The inmates of the orphanage,
The infants left to us to rear,
  State step-children of tender age,
They would describe how much is done
For children who belong to none.

If they could speak they might compare
  The Guardians with the Magistrates,
And how Home Office orphans fare,
  And how those charged upon the rates —
But Bumble sees no need to teach
These pauper waifs their native speech.

If they could reason, they would learn
  That for the wealth the State expends,
The Treasury gets no return,
  Society no dividends.
The system they would not condemn,
When everything is done for them.

They would discover they possess
  No fundamental human right
To wellbeing, health and happiness,
  To playtime, schooling, sun and light.
Expenses must not be increased
For children of the poor, deceased.

The infant concentration camp
Is all the Treasury affords,
Which leaves an everlasting stamp
On National and Council wards.
Once sentenced to protective care,
They live and breathe a prison air.

Must England rear these children so?
And are not children England's need?
And must these State step-children grow
A wretched, warped, Satanic breed?
Satanic youth! the judges say —
Who are Satanic, we or they?

## TRALALAIKA

Stalin now has at his command a fair amount of English; he can —
and occasionally does — interrupt his interpreter with 'So what?' 'What
the hell goes on here?' and 'No, sir!' *Daily Mail* on Crimea Conference, February 13th.

Yalta happy landing,
Charter of the Three,
Perfect understanding —
Why did they agree?
Down in the Crimea
All were polyglot;
Three with one idea —
Harashó! So what?

*Tra, la, tralalaika,*
*Harashó! So what?*

Churchill said they needed
No interpreter,
Roosevelt thought as he did,
*Nyet, moi dróog.* No, sir!
Warm trilateral greetings,
Secrets there were none,
Confidential meetings —
What the hell's going on?

*Tra, la, tralalaika,*
*What the hell's going on?*

Yalta ice was broken,
Heart-to-hearts began,
Basic Russki spoken
Sped the post-war plan;
Close co-ordination,
Order of the Day,
Crimea Declaration,
Harashó! O.K.!

*Tra, la, tralalaika,*
*Harashó! O.K.!*

# THE ROOT OF THE TROUBLE

General de Gaulle has been resting at his home, following dental
treatment. — News Item, *Manchester Guardian*.

The reason may now be disclosed
  Why France rebuffed Roosevelt's 'come hither — '
Her most sensitive nerve was exposed,
  And her best friends could do nothing with her.
The venom that seemed to be working
  They could not locate nor control
Till poison was found to be lurking
  At the root of the tooth of de Gaulle.

Now France to the General defers
  As her saviour, her head and defender,
So it follows his toothache is hers
  When the nerves of the General are tender.
His pangs must arouse indignation
  Which poisons relations Allied,
And the General's advanced inflammation
  Inflamed France's national pride.

The American crisis acute
  Redoubled de Gaulle's self-assertion,
But the trouble when traced to the root
  Was not shown as a rooted aversion.
Though while France and de Gaulle kept their distance
  And behaved in a manner uncouth
The American Entente's existence
  Might be said to have hung by a tooth.

But goodwill by toothache obscured
   Is more lasting than poisoned affection,
And the crisis by dentistry cured
   Only needed a local injection.
No poisonous aims were imputed,
   No venom has seared France's soul,
And the root of the trouble's uprooted
   With the root of the tooth of de Gaulle.


## ALLONS, CAMERADOS
### [*After Walt Whitman*]

Allons, camerados, en route for *libertad*,
Forward to the horizon endlessly stretching,
Camerados of all climes, colours, races, occupations, latitudes,
Habitans of all classes enlisted indiscriminately,
Camerados of the wartime world, supernumerary Field Marshals,
    political generals, strategist statesmen,
Business bosses commanding multitudinous proletarians,
Higher income groups and lower income groups,
Allons the march of democracy.

In the van, idealist-realist Americanos leading,
Cheek by jowl with, but slightly ahead of, realist-idealists of Britain,
Allons, camerados, processioning from the West plenteously teeming.
Realizing the ideal in the terms of *realidad*,
Allons, laden with mass-produced manufactures on easy terms,
Automobiles, frigidaires, radios, washing machines,
Allons over battlefields and devastations.

Charters, White Papers, Declarations, protocols scattering,
Under an umbrella of psychological leaflets,
Democracy's *feuillage*
Passports of *libertad*.

140

Forward, multitudes exurging into the future,
Allons over the corpses of enemies and kinsmen,
Ordered Democracy trampling the desperados of Democracy;
Every defeated land is a competitor out of the ring,
Every liberated country a market-to be,
Allons, industrial civilization with markets ever expanding.
'The greed that with perfect complaisance devours all things',
Allons, camerados, to transitional victory,
Allons to victorious transition.


## ACCIDENT IN THE ALLIED CAMP

*[After Robert Browning]*

American troops of General Hodges' First Army crossed the Rhine,
March 8th, 1945.

You know Remagen Bridge was seized
        A week or two ago —
The High Command was hardly pleased,
        It almost wrecked the show.
The bridge they thought as good as blown
        When Ike's assault began;
Allied Headquarters had their own
        Supreme strategic plan.

Although their plan did not neglect
        The crossing of the Rhine.
Remagen Bridge should have been wrecked
        According to design;
Though an objective had been won,
        They felt acute dismay,
For things in warfare are not done
        In this haphazard way.

SHAEF's courier galloped to the ridge
    Where Hodges with his troop
Stood looking on Remagen Bridge,
    And cried 'Regroup, regroup!
The spearheads that advance too far
    Imperil all the flank —
Blow yonder bridge while yet you are
    Upon the western bank.

The whole concerted war machine
    Together must advance,
You dare not take an unforeseen
    And accidental chance.
The Field Commander must not flout
    The Allies' master plan;
SHAEF will arrange a news blackout —
    Retire now while you can.'

O then the eagle eyes flashed fire
    Above that scene of strife,
And General Hodges barked 'Retire?
    No, not on your sweet life!
Great snakes! I've crossed the Rhine', he cried,
    'There lies our first bridgehead'.
And sinking at the General's side,
    The man from SHAEF fell dead.

# MOH-SHE-HEH-MOEE

Lord Halifax has been made a member of the Osage Indian tribe and was given the name of Mohsheshemoee — an-eagle-flying-above-the-clouds. — News Item.

Who cruises high above the clouds?
   Moh-she-heh-moee.
Who soars beyond the eagle crowds?
   Moh-she-heh-moee.
When braves across Salt Water sail
To blaze the New World sunrise trail,
Who sends a reassuring hail?
   Moh-she-heh-moee.

When 'Frisco council fires are lit
   Beside the peace tepee,
And peace-pipe-smoking-eagles sit
   To vote in their degree,
Who will they find already there,
Who will, far off, their councils share,
Though leagues above them in the air?
   Moh-she-heh-moee.

Big Double Eagle of the States,
   Yank-heh-dooh-dle-dee,
Will greet war-painted delegates
   For the Big Eagles three.
Some hawks of second magnitude,
Some like the common buzzard brood,
But lately raised to eaglehood —
   And Moh-she-heh-moee.

The Council, as it cranes its neck
      Above the clouds will see
A distant but inspiring speck —
      Moh-she-heh-moee.
And as each brave begins his speech,
From heights as far as eye can reach,
Will float his optimistic screech,
      Moh-she-heh-moee.

The fighting cock with eagle crest,
      Some think will disagree;
Some fear small fowl will be suppressed
      To leave Big Eagles free.
But who was lately heard to say,
This peace pow-wow will be O.K.,
Big Eagle Chiefs will see fair play?
      Moh-she-heh-moee.

## HIP! HIP! HIP! SSSH!

'There is no undue optimism in this house. We are not interested in the possibilities of lightning victory. They do not exist.'

There is *no* wishful thinking in Britain,
   *No* rise-tinted glasses are worn,
*No* victory marches are written,
   War prophets are looked on with *scorn*.
New trials are *not* underrated,
   There are *no* super-optimists here,
But the end, as of old, is awaited
   With *temperate* cheer.

*No* chickens in Britain are counted,
    Stern ordeals have still to be met,
High hurdles must still be surmounted,
    We cannot see daylight as yet.
Peace Plans are *not* so far perfected,
    As we mass for the final break-through,
And victory is *not* expected
    Before it is due.

Predictions are rightly mistrusted,
    We are *not* ahead of the clock,
The Stock Exchange must be adjusted
    For meeting the ultimate shock.
Divorced from all pleasing illusion
    Fair forecasts are out of our scope,
But we wait the predestined conclusion
    With *confident* hope.

From neutral observers we differ,
    We reckon *no* short cut to peace,
Our upper lip *never* was stiffer,
    Our wartime exertions increase.
We shun premature jubilation,
    Emotions are strictly controlled,
We will not predict the duration
    Until we are told.

Though skies are progressively brightening,
    It is futile to peer through the mist —
As for victory coming like lightning
    The likelihood does not exist;
All rumours are rigidly tested,
    War wagers are promptly refused,
And when victory sweeps are suggested,
    *We are not amused.*

## LONDON BURNING

Gone are the churches, tall watchmen of the City,
Gone are the landmarks that London used to know,
Great halls and ancient walls, fallen, warped and charred now,
Gone are the chiming steeples, cracked and jarred now,
Gone are the bookmen of Paternoster Row.

Red roared the fire through the heart of London's City,
Hurled from the clouds by a brute and savage foe,
They who their own land robbed of light and learning
Kindled the books here, a brand for London's burning,
Lighted the bonfire of Paternoster Row.

Long shall men mourn the burning of the City,
As long as London town shall stand or London's river flow,
Mourn for the treasured links with gentler ages,
Wealth of the humble, old shrines for pilgrimages,
St. Bride's and All Hallow's and Paternoster Row.

Low shall they lie, the wreckers of the City,
Great Gog and Magog will strike a triple blow;
Once for the Guildhall of worship and of fame there,
Twice for the white spires given to the flame there,
And thrice for the bookmen of Paternoster Row.

# RECITATIVE

When in this time of indubitable National emergency
The Government is faced with problems of equal magnitude and
  urgency,
When the *soi-disant* Ministry of Home Security, (of which it can give
  not the slightest assurance),
Exhorts the bombarded populace to further miracles of fortitude and
  endurance
Because the War Office, despite the allocation of incalculable millions,
Fails to prevent the brunt of enemy action falling exclusively upon
  civilians;
When the numerous Departments of Circumlocution with incom-
  parable agility
Evade the assumption of joint, mutual or individual responsibility,
While doing more to retard the country's War Effort in export trade
  production
Than a month of intensive air raids despite their widely advertised
  mass destruction,
And when we see how officialdom in the name of national safety can
  with complete impunity,
Harass, badger, hamstring and paralyze the productive half of the
  community,
We realize that not only the countries roughly classified and thoroughly
  detested as autarchical,
But also our own, immemorially extolled as a Constitutionally
  monarchical,
Universally enfranchised and politically educated Parliamentary
  Democracy,
May be likewise the helpless victim of a flatulent, piddling, arbitrary,
  obstructionist and imbecile Bureaucracy.

*October* 1940

## WAR-FARE

They cook the news
At G.H.Q.s,
They flavour at B.U.P.,
They hang till high
At the M.O.I.
And they serve through the B.B.C.

## BRITAIN CAN TAKE IT

Night-raiding bombers rain
    Death and destruction,
Britain builds up again,
    Speeds war production;
White-hot her purpose glows,
    Nothing can shake it,
Hardened by hammer blows
    Britain can take it.

Hark to the Treasury
    Calling up War Loans,
War Bonds for victory,
    More loans and more loans,
Every pound they will spend
    Fast as we make it,
No matter *what* we lend
    Britain can take it.

Railways are all employed
    Serving the nation,
Doubling fares to avoid
    Vicious inflation;

148

Transport's full steam ahead,
　　Nothing can brake it,
Well have the Railways said,
　　'Railways can take it.'

Will there be price control?
　　At the first rumour,
Corner the market whole,
　　Skin the consumer;
Britons on Britons prey,
　　Never mistake it,
Britain must pay and pay,
　　Britons will take it.

Britain can only win
　　Through sacrifices,
Vast the war effort in
　　Piling up prices;
Once they have heard the call
　　None will forsake it,
There is no doubt at all
　　Britons can take it.

*December* 1940

# WALKING IN THE BLACK-OUT, 1940

## [*After John Gay*]

When Heav'n's celestial Queen withdraws her Light,
Shun London Pavements in the dang'rous Night
Where Stygian Darkness and the jostling Crowd
The Step bewilder and the Sense becloud.
Pil'd Sandbags trip you if in haste you go,
You tempt Pickpockets if your Pace be slow,
While Light Restrictions still your Progress vex
Though half the Population break their Necks.
Beside the Kerb the doubtful Walker stands,
Crossing he takes his Life within his Hands;
Late for the Play, beneath a Bus he falls
While anxious Cronies wait him in the Stalls.
By London Transport at his Tryst delayed,
The Lover strays in Mayfair's noxious Shade,
By wav'ring Torchlight caught in Silken Snares
He's lured by guileful Harlots to their Lairs.
The modest Female, fluster'd by the Dark
Mistakes Pall Mall and roves beside the Park;
Her lonely state inflames the Rake's desires,
Her Screams unheard, of Terror she expires.
Then, Reader, Life and Virtue risk no more
But hang the Almanac behind the Door,
Pass moonless Nights in conjugal Retreat
Till Cynthia's Beams engild the silver'd Street,
And when her Rays once more on Earth are strown,
Step out and seek the Pleasures of the Town.

# APOLOGIA

We know of course that beggars can't be choosers,
We know when drowning one must clutch at straws,
Allies we need if we would not be losers,
And dare not probe too deep for moral flaws;
But large crusading hosts of thugs and bruisers
Must always faintly prejudice the cause,
Our history having recently recorded
Some aid may be too dear to be afforded.

While lacking an authoritative voice
To state our aims for general restitution,
(We pay our money and we take our choice
Clear from the *status quo* to revolution)
Still we can unaffectedly rejoice
That certain States have made no contribution;
So we in triumph need not be appeasers
Of modern Attilas and pseudo Caesars.

To virtue we may have but small pretension,
But somewhere everyone must draw the line,
And with wholehearted thankfulness we mention,
No, more, with rapture words cannot define,
Our offer of untimely intervention
Rumania thought proper to decline,
Or we might have been called upon to rescue
The Iron Guard and Mr. Antonescu.

It's also not a little gratifying,
Though more by luck than management perhaps,
We have not been obliged to swear undying
Devotion to the 'gallant little Japs'.

Since propagandists must have found it trying
To bridge some manifestly awkward gaps
In making us appear the willing votary
Of Prince Konoye and his revolting coterie!

True, we were long compelled, postponing war,
To treat with the offscourings of humanity,
But none the less continued to deplore
Each blow at justice, truth and Christianity,
The worst that can be laid at Britain's door
Is trustfulness just verging on insanity —
We may have had a touch of Halifaxis,
We are at least a cut above the Axis!

*January* 1941


## CHERCHEZ LA FEMME
[*After Autin Dobson*]

The tradition of highly-placed mistresses and their participat on in
politics is an ancient one in France. Both M. Reynaud and M. Daladier
figure in relationships with calculating women . . . the Countess
Hélène de Portes and the Marquise de Crussol. — *Report on France.*
*Thomas Kernan.*

> When the fall of France was brewing,
> *Belle comtesse*,
> Did you work for her undoing
> With success?
> Were her strong men all too human,
> Premier R and Monsieur D?
> They who choose to 'find the woman'
> Find yourself, Comtesse de P
> (So disguised for *politesse*).

Did you mix, with skill supreme,
Statecraft with *la vie intime*
As in *l'ancien régime*,
*Belle comtesse?*

Had the Cabinet *une crise*
Every time you staged a breeze
With your rival, *la marquise:*
Eh, *comtesse?*
Were you to *la France* a pain?
Were you Monsieur R's *migraine?*
Did he rule and did you reign,
*Belle comtesse?*
Were you merely in due season
Used by master-minds of treason?
France fell, but were you the reason,
*Belle comtesse?*

In her tale of woe and grief,
*Belle comtesse,*
You appear as light relief,
More or less;
Were the ills of France, past cure,
Insufficient, to be sure?
Must we add to these *l'amour,*
*Belle comtesse?*

*February* 1941

153

# FILIBUSTER

Administration leaders now accuse isolationists of being engaged in a 'filibuster' ... A 'filibuster' is generally regarded as beginning when senators read from an encyclopaedia. — *Manchester Guardian*, March 4th, 1941.

By the shore of the Potomac
Sit the prophets of the nation,
Like the rocks with mosses on them,
Holding up the Lend and Lease Bill,
Aid for Greece and aid for Britain.
Isolation's filibusters
Holding up the swift destroyers,
Holding up the long-range bombers.
Very old is filibustering,
Very old and democratic,
Very full of repetition.
Ninety days, or maybe sixty,
See Democracy in death-throes,
While the prophets of the nation
Cry they hear the war-drums beating,
While the Axis marches eastward,
While the Axis marches southward,
While the dwindling British convoys
Founder in the wide Atlantic.
Still the Senators hold pow-wow,
Sixty days, or maybe ninety,
Hearing Nye of North Dakota,
Hearing Wheeler of Montana,
And la Follette of Wisconsin
Calling up the shade of Borah,
Late of Idaho, at present
In eternal isolation
In the Land of the Hereafter.

When, to kill the Lend and Lease Bill,
When they wander off the subject,
Reading from the Book of Numbers,
Reading the Encyclopaedia
Clear from ANNO through to ZYGO,
Then it is they filibuster,
Keeping up the old tradition,
Crabbing the Administration,
By the shore of the Potomac.


## HUSTLE

The visiting American technical man finds difficulty in establishing quick and effective contact with the operative section of the appropriate department in Whitehall for obtaining action in a given sphere of the war effort. — *Daily Telegraph*, March 18th, 1941.

Mr. X, I'm delighted to meet you,
You bring timely assistance indeed,
But Lord Y could not stay in to greet you
And I can't tell you how to proceed.
For material leased, loaned and rented
We have no authority here;
Your inquiries should not be presented
Till you find the appropriate sphere.

We will work for full co-ordination,
But your Bill was so suddenly signed
That for maximum implementation
Our machinery is somewhat behind.
Great Britain's own wartime production
We've had too little time to prepare,
So we're switched to post-war reconstruction
And to-day my Chief's taking the Chair.

I've heard that a branch was deputed
To deal with American aid,
But the office has been devoluted
And liaison has still to be made.
Your contact will soon be effected
With an operative section no doubt,
And I'm trying to get you connected
But everyone seems to be out.

In regard to the present position
I'm afraid that I can't help you much;
If you cable our Purchasing Mission
I am sure they will put you in touch.
Lord Y will regret that he missed you
When he hears in due course of your call.
And I'm sorry I cannot assist you
But we're busy to-day in Whitehall.


## BLOW THE MAN DOWN

Further details of the enormous exports of goods from France to
Germany were made known in London yesterday. From the middle
of January until March 1st, French railways in unoccupied France
carried to Germany 38,000 tons of bauxite, 10,000 tons of aluminium,
8,000 tons of magnesium, 30,000 tons of wool, 2,200 tons of Chilean
nitrates, 60,000 tons of fruit, and 1,700 tons of rubber. The railways
in occupied France carried 77,000 tons of raw materials 'important for
the war' and therefore marked by the Germans for 'absolute priority'
in transport. — *The Times*, April 1st, 1941.

Oh, as we kept watch for the enemy fleet,
*Way-ay blow the man down!*
Some warships from Vichy we happened to meet,
*Give us some time to blow the man down.*

Sez they 'We will thank you to pass through the Straits,
*Way-ay blow the man down!*
For we're westbound to Dakar for peanuts and dates',
*Give us some time to blow the man down.*

So we stands off politely and passes them through,
*Way-ay blow the man down!*
With a *Parlez vous Vichy* and How d'you do?
*Give us some time to blow the man down.*

As we were a-watching for war contraband,
*Way-ay blow the man down!*
Some Frenchies creeps past in the lee of the land,
*Give us some time to blow the man down.*

'Oh where are you bound for and whence do you come?'
*Way-ay blow the man down!*
'We're for France with a load of bananas and rum',
*Give us some time to blow the man down.*

So we rightabout turns and they sails on their way,
*Way-ay blow the man down!*
Though we sailors have got no bananas to-day,
*Give us some time to blow the man down.*

For we stops every vessel a-sailing the sea,
*Way-ay blow the man down!*
But hands off the freight for the port of Vichee,
*Give us some time to blow the man down.*

And the Nazi sez he when the voyage is made,
*Way-ay blow the man down!*
'*Gott und Darlan sei Dank* for the British blockade!'
*Give us some time to blow the man down.*

Stalin made a surprise appearance at the station when Matsuoka was preparing to leave . . . The two statesmen were overcome by emotion and embraced each other. Most significant was the remark made by Stalin in parting: 'You are Asiatic, so am I.' — *Asahi Shimbun*, April 27th, 1941.

When Stalin popped down to the station to kiss Matsuoka good-bye
With a warmth that is seldom engendered by a common Neutrality
    Pact,
The entourage, schooled to surprises, all caught themselves wondering
    why,
And the highest Intelligence Circles could not state how the world
    would react.

When Stalin embraced Matsuoka with hardly controllable tears,
The world, which awaits new alignments with settled and justified
    gloom,
Remarked, if these boy-friends united to banish their mutual fears,
It must be against someone for something, and if so, for what, against
    whom?

By one smack on the station at Moscow all Far-Eastern issues were
    raised,
The kiss in relation to China the experts set out to define,
And Communists all the world over, already perceptibly dazed,
Awaited in mute acquiescence their cue for a sound Party line.

But the Soviet's subsequent action set wild speculation at rest.
This sign of impulsive affection was merely a matter of race,
Untouched by the fathomless cunning of the weird and inscrutable
    West,
It was Asia bestowing on Asia a non-ideologic embrace.

For even the Sphinx of the Kremlin is frequently lonesome and glum,
By comrades too long disappointed, by foreigners sadly perplexed,
Herr Ribbentrop, sometimes a caller, has never seemed, somehow, a
  chum,
And the closest of Soviet advisers may need purging by Saturday next.

And though Britain with buoyant endeavour seeks to rival the charm
  of Japan,
Cripps is never asked round to the Kremlin to sit down and have a
  good cry,
Since he's neither Siberian nor Mongol in the ethnic division of Man
Stalin will not pop down to the station to kiss Britain's envoy good-
  bye.


## FORCED LANDING

O Hess has come down like a bolt from the blue,
And nobody sent him and nobody knew,
By no one commissioned, by no one enticed,
(It takes one for a landing but two for a tryst)
He had only a map and a name and address,
There was never a fluke like the coming of Hess.

So timely he crashed near to Dungavel Hall,
Where no one expected his coming at all,
His letters unanswered, unguessed his design,
All the Scots that he knew were the words auld lang syne,
But his landing occasioned old friends no distress —
None were ever acquainted with vice-fuehrer Hess.

So costly his clothing, his manners so nice,
He had plainly no truck with a régime of vice,
News Bulletins blushed to allude to his crimes,
He was washed white as snow in the ink of the *Times*,
His horror of bloodshed words could not express —
No ace was the equal of gentleman Hess.

We are armed against Nazi assaults from the air,
For peace-flights of Nazis we now must prepare,
We know what we hear but none say what they know,
And luckier envoys may still come and go,
But even appeasers are bound to confess
There was never a flop like the peace-flight of Hess.

*May* 1941

RUBÁIYÁT

Now the new season brings the tourist trade,
From Cairo to Teheran behold displayed
The arts and crafts of all the Middle East
Both old and new and partially decayed.

Inönü in the Istanbul bazaar
Vends unrepeatable *objets d'art*,
And Rashid Ali cries his Bagdad wares,
Echoed by Abdul Illah from afar.

In Egypt's booths no price is held too high
For genuine Faroukian papyri,
And lo! beside the oil-jars of Iran
Hear Reza Shah Pahlevi call 'Come buy!'

And those who come with sacks of minted gold
To bargain in the market-place, behold,
That which they purchased was already bought,
And nothing, but the buyer, has been sold.

The more the merchants are sold out, the more
They sell without diminishing their store,
The selfsame articles will be on view
To-morrow as they were the day before.

Red Turkey carpet, stale Rahat Lakoum,
The flowers of friendship, slightly past their bloom,
Seals, talismans and old Arabian tales
Sold and re-sold — the question is, to whom?

*May* 1941


# LITTLE ENEMY ACTIVITY

The Mother of Parliaments has once more rejected the plea for
family allowances.—*News Item.*

When the Nazi might is shattered
By our armament titanic,
And the world, though slightly battered,
Rescued from the hordes Germanic,
All our hopes may be defeated
By a more deep-rooted danger,
And our progeny unseated
By the little Nazi stranger,
Though we know the whole creation
Insufficiently commodious
For a rising generation
So exceptionally odious.
While the foe we may outdistance
In the engines of destruction
They imperil our existence
By their baby mass-production,
And if Britons still diminish
While the Nazis still re-double,
We may question at the finish
If the war was worth the trouble.

For while Britain's lawful-wedded
State in converse confidential
That no prospect is more dreaded
Than their parenthood potential,
Nazi Hausfraus ever busy
Charge again the bulging cradle,
Rivalling the record dizzy
Of expectant Hitler Mädel,
While the German State and Party
Trends to race-decline have mastered,
And extend a welcome hearty
To the little Nazi bastard,
And conceive a mass-offensive
For our ultimate submersion
By the fostering·intensive
Of progenitive exertion.
Can we face so grave a peril
Or a future more horrific
If the civilized are sterile
While the savage is prolific?
With our numbers still declining
What avails our moral merit,
If the world of our designing
Little Nazis shall inherit?

*June* 1941

When Russia by the Reich attacked
Concludes the Anglo-Soviet pact,
This suddenly accomplished fact
Disposes of the 'isms';
The slogan and the shibboleth,
So powerfully talked to death,
Becoming just a waste of breath
And mere anachronisms.

Aggression by a single stroke
Collective action can provoke
(The snag on which Geneva broke,
For diplomats too tricky),
So capitalist circles here,
Forgetting their habitual fear,
Encourage with a Tory cheer
The battling Bolsheviki.

And as the *Internationale*
Keeps up the Carlton Club's morale,
While Reds hobnob with *Kapital*
Regardless of the label,
Both parties under arms dismiss
That ideologic prejudice
Which ought to be (but never is)
Discarded round a table.

This strange but logical event
Proves dead Geneva's argument
And makes its truth self-evident
To minds the most defective —

Faced with the common enemy
Extremes must as allies agree,
For there is no security
Unless it is collective.

*June* 1941


## THE MORNING AFTER

When the streets are a glimmer of grey
And distances fade from sight,
Then London goes home for the day,
And the bombers come out for the night.

And *Raiders Over* the sirens wail
With a warning, warbling sound,
And down the fire-bombs fall like hail,
And all night long till the east turns pale
The Defiant is hot on the Heinkel's tail
And the sky is a battleground.

The raider keeps hovering over your roof,
And you doubt if your basement is quite bombproof
As he hums and circles and drones and dives
And whistlers come over your head in fives,
And was that a bomb or was it a gun?
Is that one of ours now, or is it a Hun?
Here comes a screamer, the end of all!
You can't be hit *if you hear it fall!*
And you're flat on your face with the force of the blast
And the whole world's blown to bits.
Then the All Clear signals the *Raiders Passed*,
And dawn is bright in the sky at last,
And you don't find nearly so many hits
The morning after the Blitz.

164

When darkness dwindles away
The birds of prey take flight,
And London comes out for the day,
And the bombers slink home for the night.

The milk and the postman arrive at the door,
Front doors in the home front-line,
And London stands where it stood before
At work in the bright sunshine.
There's the shiver and tinkle of broken glass,
And here's a corner you cannot pass,
And here's a crater and there's a mine,
And your bus goes round if it can't go through,
Or you've got to walk (and you get there, too)
And girls troop out in the glittering air
With bright spring jackets and turbaned hair.
And if people ask how we carry on
When this is gutted and that is gone,
And face the round of a working day
Trim and jaunty and grim and gay —
Well, Londoners know that they'll be quits
*One* morning after the Blitz.

# ENFANT TERRIBLE

The Russian system is hated all over Britain. — Sir Ronald Cross.

Although right-minded Britons hate
The system of the Soviet State,
A scene they cannot contemplate
Without an inward groan,
The proletarian Russian folk
Who grunt and sweat beneath the yoke
Can yet a striking power invoke
Almost to match our own.

The Soviet worker toils and fights
According to his godless lights,
And for his economic rights
Does not appear to care,
And though his life we cannot praise,
Despite his atheistic ways,
That scorn of worldly goods displays
Which makes our lives a prayer.

For all his impious ideal,
Such is his communistic zeal
His Government need not appeal
For willing hearts and hands;
He never seems to weigh the price
When asked for total sacrifice,
A course against all sound advice
In less fanatic lands.

His savings he does not invest
In bonds and loans at interest,
His war-drive he does not arrest
To further private greed,

166

He takes the unenlightened view
The Soviet State will see him through,
And everyone receive his due
According to his need.

He is so certain of their aims,
He gives his homestead to the flames
Without first putting in his claims,
His reason is so dull,
His slogan as he carries on
Is One for All and All for One,
In his outlandish lexicon
Is no such word as lull.

And, single-minded to a fault,
He hurls his body down to halt
A hitherto unchecked assault,
While all his actions tell
He knows what he is fighting for;
So, though the thought may be a bore,
If he should chance to win the war
He wins the peace as well.

*July* 1941


IT ALL DEPENDS ON ME

When Cato strode the streets alive
And gave the Romans his opinion,
He organized a one-man drive
Against the peril Cartheginian;
Preventive action he desired,
A cultural and trade embargo,
Till everyone was sick and tired
He cried: 'Delenda est Carthago!'

He feared for Roman life and laws
Beneath a Punic occupation
(And so expressed himself because
Rome had a classic education),
But all that Cato really meant
Was, peace can never be enjoyed
If Powers are on world-conquest bent,
So Nazidom must be destroyed.

When Cato was the soul of Rome,
Both in the Senate and the Forum,
When dining out or when at home,
He harped upon Pax Romanorum;
If with patricians he conversed,
Or with the plebs in Latin *argot*,
He always got in last or first,
'I say, Delenda est Carthago!'

And now wherever you may be,
Who face a far more active danger,
Lift up your voice in company,
Or buttonhole the perfect stranger.
For pleasure or for business met,
Though people may become annoyed,
Do not let anyone forget
That Nazidom must be destroyed.

Old Cato was a ruthless bore,
Though his approach was of the blandest,
But still, he got his Punic War,
That ancient high-powered propagandist;
A case at law he would cut short,
Or philosophical farrago,
And to all argument retort,
'So what? Delenda est Carthago!'

And now though conversation stray
To different topics altogether,
Just add to anything you say
On bridge, or film stars or the weather,
Or modern girls or Handel's Largo,
Or swing bands or the unemployed,
'Likewise; Delenda est Carthago!
The Nazi State must be destroyed!'

# ONWARD, COMPARATIVELY CHRISTIAN SOLDIERS!

Onward, Christian soldiers,
Armed for total war,
Crescent moon and sickle
Going on before.
Strengthening defences,
Girding for the fight,
Westward, help comes slowly,
Eastward, it is bright!

Onward, Marxist armies,
Mainly infidel,
Smite the hordes of Wotan,
Ram the gates of Hell!
Onward, hosts of Allah
Over desert sand,
Paladins of Siva
From India's coral strand!

Onward, Afric's warriors,
Marching in the van,
Polytheists fighting
As polytheists can!

169

Moslem, Sikh and Hindu,
Bringing victory near,
Onward, Christian soldiers
Bringing up the rear!

Gather, piebald legions
Of every faith or none,
For the powers of darkness
Conquer one by one.
Satan's ranks will scatter,
Wotan's swarm depart,
Chased by Christian soldiers,
Once they make a start.

*September* 1941


# L'APRÈS-MIDI D'UN FOREIGN OFFICE FAUNE

### [*After Swinburne*]

When the foreign envoy his steps retraces,
Who spoke with Fascists in sweet accord,
One sees how well, on a friendly basis,
The pre-war footing may be restored;
Where gentle pressure has been exerted,
The breach is healed and the slip averted,
And the cliché sounds in the windy places,
While shady avenues are explored.

One feels firm rulers should be befriended,
And subjects guided by powers above,
So olive branches should be extended,
One flies the kite and sets free the dove.

Some hasty matches are ill-assorted,
The new love's wed, but the old love's courted,
Till the new world's made and the old world mended
By the flabby hand in the velvet glove.

How can we sing to them, what can we play to them,
The Moslem belt and the Latin Block?
How can we bolster them, what can we pay to them,
How can we soften the Bolshevik shock?
How Axis lovers to tame and tether,
Keep the Left apart and the Right together,
How much can we keep and how much give away to them,
Nor risk a split on the Soviet rock?

One builds afresh on the old foundations,
One dallies hidden from prying eyes,
One seeks improvements of strained relations
With old attachments, the foe's allies;
With the lords of Spain, and the royal Bulgar,
With the kings of Islam (but not the vulgar)
While treating with well-rewarded patience
The prince that follows, the Shah that flies.

*September* 1941

# THE PELICAN

Among the city's honoured names,
The tenantry of blitzed St. James',
For keeping cool amid the flames
All should commend the pelican.

Those things that often after dark
Come swishing through St. James's Park,
Wherever else they leave their mark
Can't break or bend the pelican.

The flying plinth, the molten lump,
The foreign body going bump,
Which might make Nelson's column jump
Do not up-end the pelican.

Upon his interesting face
Of nervous strain there is no trace;
The gaping of the populace
Will not offend the pelican.

Firm as a pillar of the State,
His appetite does not abate,
Fish, taken by the hundredweight
Do not distend the pelican.

Calm on his fortress isle he sits,
Between the misses and the hits;
For moral beating of the Blitz
Who can transcend the pelican?

# LULLABY

Now a lull broods in the west,
It is not the time to act;
Mention of widespread unrest
Shows a want of public tact.
Where our island ramparts rise
Long-term Blitzkriegs we prepare;
We are safe against surprise,
Good-night children, everywhere.

Bottle-necks will now be eased,
There is danger in delay,
Every ounce of effort squeezed,
Only Whitehall in the way.
Ministers have things in hand,
There's not one whom we can spare;
Everything is being planned.
Good-night children, everywhere.

Though our labour must restore
All at Dunkirk left behind,
All our arms for total war,
Let this fact be borne in mind;
We left nothing that could be,
Thanks to foresight all too rare,
Helpful to the enemy.
Good-night children, everywhere.

With invasion looming near
Confidence must be renewed;
There is cause for reasoned fear,
None for deep disquietude.

Risks in war should not be run.
Heed no unofficial scare.
Everything is being done.
Good-night children, everywhere.

*November* 1941


## HAPPY BIRTHDAY TO YOU

The B.B.C. broadcast good wishes to the King of Italy on his
birthday. — November 11th, 1941.

The Government told England we were in a state of war,
They told why we were fighting and what we were fighting for,
They notified the neutrals and they told the enemy,
But they never told the B.B.C.

They told the non-belligerents, though the statement was deferred,
They told the Foreign Office, though we don't know if they heard,
They told the British Commonwealth who hastened to agree,
But they never told the B.B.C.

They told the British Army and they told the T.U.C.,
They wired the Royal Navy wherever it might be,
But they failed to give the matter nation-wide publicity,
For they never told the B.B.C.

They told the Nazi leaders they must answer for their crimes,
They told the penny papers and they even told *The Times*,
They pumped out propaganda through a special Ministry,
But they never told the B.B.C.

In consequence, while waiting the official news release,
The B.B.C. concluded we were in a state of peace,
So they broadcast birthday greetings to the King of Italy;
For they never told the B.B.C.

So the Government decided, though the process has been slow,
It was in the public interest that the B.B.C. should know,
And somebody has taken full responsibility
And they're going to tell the B.B.C.

## HABITATION OF BITTERNS

'. . . when London shall be an habitation of bitterns, when St. Paul's
and Westminster Abbey shall stand, shapeless and nameless ruins in the
midst of an unpeopled marsh . . .' — Shelley.

If London were the bittern's habitation,
A nameless and illimitable fen,
Become through transatlantic mass-migration
An empty and unpeopled marsh again;
If nettles throve in Whitehall's howling spaces,
If Piccadilly were a place of skulls
And nothing visited the market places
But sparrows and the pigeons and the gulls,

If in the Mansion House the brown owl hooted,
If in the Law Courts, permanently cleared,
The bindweed with the willowherb disputed
And nothing moved on 'Change but old man's beard,
If heron fished beside the mere at Wapping,
If Billingsgate were fringed with osier stems,
If ouzels skimmed the silver ripples lapping
The seven broken bridges of the Thames,

Amid the universal demolition
Beneath the ivied, architectural crag
Some unrecorded human apparition
Would scatter breadcrumbs from a paper bag;
Where City sites, eternally vacated
Yawned in a solitude beyond all words,
The last of London's residents belated,
Someone would still be there to feed the birds.


# COME INTO THE ARMY, MAUD

A.T.S. Adventure Through Service. — Daily advertisement.

Come into the Army, Maud,
Your hours of ease are flown,
Get into the Army, Maud,
They are waiting for you alone,
And the word of command has been wafted abroad
And the fall-in finally blown.

You were blind to the ads. in the daily Press,
So they got you, sweet, on the run;
You would not pop into your battle-dress,
Though the War Office said it was fun;
You would not become an adventuress
In the ranks of adventurous A.T.S.,
Where brave girls cook for the Sergeants' Mess
And the batwoman busily bats.

You have failed to volunteer
So at last you have met your fate;
There has risen a splendid cheer
From the Commons holding debate.

The Air Force cried, 'She is near, she is near!'
But the War Office muttered, 'We wait!'
The Navy trolled, 'She is here, she is here!'
But the Army barked, 'She is late!'

Queen weed in the garden of Service girls,
You may sigh the whole war through
For gloss of ermine and glamour of pearls,
Or even a uniform blue.
De-rouge the nails, bind up the curls,
And into the A.T.S. with you!

*December* 1941


# TRADITIONAL

There must be far-flung outposts seized by treacherous attack,
Though every preparation has been made,
There must be overwhelming odds, with few to hold them back,
While strong relieving forces are delayed.
There must be tiny garrisons defying every threat,
Cut off from reinforcements and supplies —
Defenders of the Empire where the sun can never set
From the empire where the sun's about to rise.

Our spearheads must be cornered and the corners must be tight,
Encircled enemies must spring the trap;
The hope must always be forlorn for which our pickets fight
In rearguard actions right around the map.
Behaviour in the field must be traditionally rash,
The High Command traditionally slow;
And generals must be models of insouciance and dash,
Against the coldly calculating foe.

There must be decorations heaped on heroes of all ranks
For exploits of imperishable fame,
And full inferiority of guns, or planes, or tanks,
For which nobody at home must take the blame.
There must be gallant Governors of marked *sang froid* and poise
Who, when they bid their Colony good-bye,
Escape through tropic jungles, led by faithful native boys,
And end in armchairs at the M.O.I.

We must adhere precisely to the proper rules of war,
Though our enemies are *capable de tout,*
And, knowing they will do again what they have done before,
We must be quite astounded when they do.
We must make sure assistance is too little and too late
So the enemy at first, may win the race,
But our subterranean strategy can well afford to wait
Till in 1943 we set the pace.

We must marvel at the enemy's fanatic will to win
As successfully we disengage our force,
And grit our teeth in readiness to take it on the chin
Until the war assumes a normal course.
And if we sometimes register an unforeseen reverse
Because the foe a reckless sally dared,
We have the consolation that things might have been much worse
If the Axis had surprised us unprepared.

*December* 1941

# IF IT HAPPENED HERE

*[After Walter de la Mare]*

'Scorched earth!' says Whitehall,
'Lay waste the land,
From Weep to Wassop
Let nothing stand.
Burn the hamlets
And fire the crops,
Grimes' Long Barn
And Turvey's hops.'
Weep and Wassop
Put down their foot:
'Foes be landed,
But we stay put.
Weep folk reckon
Scorched earth may be
Right for Russians,
But not for we.
Tupman's meadow
Just under the plough,
'Twere plain foolish
To burn it now.
Wassop Manor
Be bolted and barred,
Squire baint trusting
They young Home Guard.
Parson says, if
His back was turned
Wouldn't wonder
If old church burned.
Weep's wormy timbers
Be quick to catch;
And who'd pay Snug
For his brand-new thatch?'

In Tudor tea-nook
Half-way to Weep,
Wassop's witches
Through curtains peep;
And Goody sits
In her locked-up shop
Bare of bull's-eye
And lollipop.
The guns are loud
And the church bells sound,
But Weep and Wassop
Will hold their ground.
The tanks are near
But in churchyard hole,
'Pish,' says blindworm,
And 'Tush,' says mole.


## NO COMPLACENCY

Though, after moments of suspense,
   Responsive to the master touch,
The Commons vote that confidence
   Of which they cannot show too much.
Though Ministers grow mightier yet,
   Safeguarded for all time to be,
Though Britain save her Cabinet,
   There must be no complacency.

And though in Libya's desert waste
   Our armoured thrust in circles wheels,
Our vanguard pressing on in haste,
   The foe retreating on our heels.

Though neither sandstorms, dust nor rain
    Obscure our twice-won victory,
On Cyrenaica's campaign
    There must be no complacency.

Though Britain's property out East,
    Where so much capital was spent,
Is rescued from scorched earth at least,
    And safe for post-war settlement.
Though with the Japanese defeat,
    Instead of valueless *débris*
Our goods will be restored complete,
    There must be no complacency.

Though in the arms production race,
    With battle raging at its height,
We fashion at majestic pace
    A full two-thirds of what we might,
Though trials must therefore be severe,
    Until in 1943
We may have grounds for sober cheer,
    There must be no complacency.

*January* 1942

# THE FACTS

Facts are what no one can be in possession of
Outside the Government's innermost fold,
Something that all must concur in suppression of,
Facts in their fullness must never be told.

Only the facts give a hold on reality,
Though stranger than fiction the facts could be shown,
Interested persons must learn with finality
It's not in their interest for facts to be known.

Slips diplomatic, strategic and tactical,
Unforeseen setbacks which tend to recur,
All must appear as the only course practical,
Having regard to the facts as they were.

What are the facts?  Are they incomprehensible?
Are they the cause, or the cure of our qualms?
Do they, when whispered, make people insensible?
Do they strike dumb, like the Monster of Glamis?

What are the facts?  Are they sunny or sinister?
Ignorant queries are here out of place;
All we can read is the face of a Minister
Pallid from looking the facts in the face.

All we can know is, that facts inaccessible
Govern the actions the crisis exacts;
All the decisions, however unguessable,
Will be in accordance with all of the facts.

# NO CONFIRMATION

Dense mist on the Channel is lying,
   The jungle is murkier still,
In the desert, where dust-storms are flying,
   Visibility's said to be nil.
Fog over Whitehall is terrific,
   We cannot quite see where we are,
The Japanese claim the Pacific.
   There is no confirmation so far.

We have moved to a stronger position,
   We have shortened our line for a stand,
We are ready to force a decision
   With the whole situation in hand.
Strategic retreat is completed,
   Fierce counter-attacks will begin;
The enemy's claims are repeated.
   Confirmation has not yet come in.

We are mounting a counter-offensive,
   We are holding the enemy back.
He finds it extremely expensive
   When he ventures a full-scale attack.
His lines of supply have been pounded,
   His time-table clearly upset,
He states that our force is surrounded.
   There is no confirmation as yet.

The enemy claims infiltration,
   The action as yet is obscure,
Until we receive confirmation
   Announcements would be premature.

Discount every Axis assertion,
    For ignorance always is bliss;
The Home Front relies on our version.

*There is no confirmation of this!*


# FREEDOM IS IN PERIL
## [*After Rudyard Kipling*]

We are fighting the battle of freedom in the world against great odds. Do not add to these odds by deeds which cast a doubt on the sincerity of our aims. — Lloyd George, March 24th, 1942.

When the last newspaper is printed and the ink is faded and dried,
And the oldest critic is muzzled and the youngest croaker has died,
We shall pass to a tranquil era of government by decree,
When every voice shall be silenced but the voice of the B.B.C.

We shall hearken to Government spokesmen, we shall listen to Government news;
And no one will doubt or question, and none shall express their views.
And only the good shall be favoured, and only the killjoy shall fall,
And the murmur of opposition will never be heard at all.

And only the Leader shall praise us and only the Leader shall blame,
And Parliament will be sitting, but Parliament will be tame,
And the star of freedom will vanish; we shall steer by the Fascist star,
And no one will then remember the sort of people we are.

# AFTER VICTORY

A spacious, active, enterprising, gay country after war. — Mr.
Lyttelton, April 26th, 1942.

It was a peacetime evening,
Old William's watch was done,
And he before his sandbagged cave
Was polishing his gun;
While by him scavenged on the green
The little war-child, Wavelline.

She rummaged in a refuse pile
And found a rusty tin,
Exclaiming with a thrifty smile,
'That's for the salvage bin.'
But he replied, 'No, little maid,
I'll use it for a hand-grenade.'

'But say, Old William, why you fight
Now we have won the war,
And what,' asked the redundant mite,
'Are people fighting for,
And say why must guerrillas be
After our famous victory?'

Old William answered 'Long we fought
The tyrant to resist,
It was some years before we caught
The bus that Hitler missed,
But still our long-term policy
Led us at last to victory.'

'It was not till the war was won
That fighting here began,
And practically everyone
Became a partisan;
For better worlds you cannot build
Without some people getting killed.

'The coming of the peace implied
The ending of the truce.'
'Well, then,' the captious infant cried,
'Whatever was the use?'
'Why, that I cannot tell,' said he,
'It was that kind of victory.'


## POSTSCRIPT; FAR EAST

We sent too little and too late
To save ourselves, to save the Dutch,
Because, unconscious of our fate,
We'd sold the enemy too much.


## THE WEEK'S GOOD CAUSE

The Government has accepted the criterion that vested interests cannot be allowed to stand in the way of the war effort. — Mr. Attlee, May 25th, 1942.

Comforts for coalowners,
Help, however small!
Alms for shipping magnates
Who have given all!

Pre-war profits dwindle,
Markets still decrease,
Safeguard vested interests
Against the risks of peace!

Economic justice is the first of post-war aims;
Can we be indifferent to industrialists' claims?
Jobs for British workers returning from the front,
What of capital that bore the economic brunt?

Caterers are ruined by pegging prices down,
Sixteen-shilling dinners are sold for but a crown;
Nest-eggs from the nation in all the soldiers' nests,
Take up a collection for our vested interests!

Rescue our shipowners from singing in the street,
Stripped of everything except the British Merchant Fleet.
Help our kings of industry, who never asked the price!
Bonuses for victims of unequal sacrifice!

Aid for war-contractors
Crippled by control!
Pennies for our bankers
Threatened with the dole!
Bundles for Big Business
Doomed to bankruptcy!
Won't you spare a copper
For the E.P.T.?

# THE CORAL SEA

This story of the first sailors ashore after the action in the Coral Sea is reported from an Australian port. — May 15th, 1942.

Three sailors came to The Seaman's Rest,
A roaring dockside dive
For those who go down to the sea in ships
And come back from the sea alive.

Men came and went from the humming quays
Where tramps and troopships lay;
Three sailors lifted their glasses up
And their eyes were far away.

They talked of the war in The Seaman's Rest,
Of news that was guessed or heard;
Three sailors stared at the bar-room wall
And none of them spoke a word.

They talked of the threat from the Coral Sea,
And of raiders over the town;
Three sailors lifted their glasses up
And drank, and crashed them down.

'We have come to port from the Coral Sea,
We have met with their ships of war,
And we reckoned to drink at The Seaman's Rest
If ever we got to shore.

'We have sunk their ships in the Coral Sea,
On fire from stem to stern,
And we've drunk a toast to our lost shipmates,
To those who did not return.'

# EDITORIAL

For two or three days . . . criticism of the battle was held up. You cannot have a free press and at the same time instructions to prevent optimistic statements being made. — Deputy Prime Minister, June 23rd, 1942.

Battle rages to and fro,
Baffling prediction;
Man for man we match the foe,
Such is our conviction.
Grave news from the Middle East
Is in our possession
Which must be, until released,
Handled with discretion.

Though our state might well be worse,
Outposts have retreated,
There may be a new reverse
(Reverse must be deleted).
Under desert storms and suns
Fighting grows intenser.
We have not their weight of guns
(Guns cut by the censor).

New offensives we await,
And it should be hinted
Egypt may share Libya's fate.
(Hint must not be printed.)
Our Imperial General Staff,
Now long past maturity,
May write the Empire's epitaph
(Staff censored for security).

(Reader, we may say our say
    Under general warning.
We may well be here to-day,
    And gone to-morrow morning.
Reader, England's Press is free,
    But the Editorial
Must be thus, lest it should be
    The Editor's memorial.)


# THE PASSIONATE PROFITEER TO HIS LOVE

*[After Christopher Marlow]*

Come feed with me and be my love,
And pleasures of the table prove,
Where *Prunier* and *The Ivy* yield
Choice dainties of the stream and field.

At *Claridge* thou shalt duckling eat,
Sip vintages both dry and sweet,
And thou shalt squeeze between thy lips
Asparagus with buttered tips.

On caviare my love shall graze,
And plump on salmon mayonnaise,
And browse at *Scott's* beside thy swain
On lobster Newburg with champagne.

Between hors d'œuvres and canapés
I'll feast thee on *poularde soufflé*
And every day within thy reach
Pile melon, nectarine and peach.

Come share at the *Savoy* with me
The menu of austerity;
If in these pastures thou wouldst rove
Then feed with me and be my love.


## SALMAGANDHI

India faces annihilation,
Gandhi speaks of the common cause,
Gandhi vetoes co-operation,
Worse will come if the Raj withdraws.
India seethes in the painful pause,
Delhi stiffens and Congress leans,
Gandhi offers an explanation —
Nobody knows what Gandhi means.

Who is losing the war, who winning,
British India knows not, nor heeds,
The bonds are snapped and the end beginning,
India follows where Gandhi leads.
Azad argues and Nehru pleads,
The Axis dangles a glittering bait —
Waiting for light sits Gandhi spinning,
Spinning the thread of India's fate.

Gulfs are yawning and parties splitting,
Councillors reason and Liberals plan;
Wherever the Moslem League is sitting
Clear is the word of the Mussulman.
Peace at the price of Pakistan,
Or the final blow at the Raj is dealt,
All compromise with the Hindu hitting —
Hitting below the Moslem belt.

Plain is the Government condition,
Plain is the meaning of Ambedkar,
Plain is the interim proposition
Of Rajagopalachariar;
Clear speak the Princes in Durbar,
Clear is the standpoint of Subhas Bhose,
Clear are the terms of the British Mission —
Gandhi's meaning nobody knows.

India must suffer armed protection,
Britain must go by polite request,
Troops must be shunned like the plague infection,
By the highest caste and the most depressed;
Hamstrung Britain must do her best
With the wheels slowed down and the land unploughed —
Mahatma Gandhi gives direction,
Spinning the thread for India's shroud.

*July* 1942


## MATTHEW ARNOLD WRITES TO
## *THE LISTENER*

On the night of May 31st the broadcast of the nightingale was accompanied by the sound of the thousand bombers setting out for Cologne.

Hark! ah, the nightingale,
Somewhere in Surrey!
Listen, Eugenia, to the radio!
What melody! — what else?

O wanderer from classic times,
Still dost thou harp on that antique event,
Thy mythological metamorphosis
In lonely Daulis and the Thracian wild —
Ignoring time and change,
This English garden-copse,
The leaf-hung microphone,
The trellised 'cellist nigh,
Thine audience unseen?
Dost thou not hear to-night
Metallic Furies in mechanic flight,
The brazen-bowelled harpies overhead,
Stretched wings, unfeathered breasts,
With open throttles roaring out above
Thy relatively sequestered solitude?
Canst thou mourn on,
Embroidering thine old-world threnody,
Oblivious of their note, as they of thine,
While my racked nerves and brain,
Disturbed in cultivated meditation
By this cacophonous phenomenon,
Apotheosis of our modern life,
Can find no balm?
Thou canst! again — Eugenia!
What bursts! what drones! what incongruity!
Eternal fixity!
Eternal flux!

# ANCIEN RÉGIME

[*After Thomas Hardy*]

We who have steered the ship of state,
Gentlemen,
Now hear the call to abdicate.
We listen for our exit cue,
You bid us leave the stage, but then,
We read the signs as well as you,
Gentlemen.

We have conducted for the best,
Gentlemen,
Our own (and Britain's) interest.
Her plans and policies were ours,
We spoke for every citizen,
We wrestled with aggressor Powers,
Gentlemen.

Through thick and thin we always were
Gentlemen.
We have borne burdens many a year,
By Baldwin led, and Chamberlain
Who braved the gangsters in their den
For Abyssinia, Munich, Spain,
Gentlemen.

We leave our mark upon the war
Gentlemen,
In Burma, India, Singapore.
Through peace and strife we carry on,
What we have done we'd do again;
We need not fear oblivion,
Gentlemen.

Youth will be served; our days decline,
Gentlemen.
The Left invites us to resign.
No day dawns twice; the tide is flowing,
The future lies beyond our ken.
But all the same, we are not going,
Gentlemen.


## LATIN BLOCKHEADS

Anglo-Spanish relations are, in fact, about as good as they could be
under existing circumstances . . . Sir Samuel Hoare . . . has certainly
performed a difficult mission surprisingly well. — *Observer*, August
30th, 1942.

There are no neutrals in a people's war
As in old wars of thrones and dynasties,
And diplomatic feints avail no more
When multitudes against their tyrants rise.
We fight a people's victory to gain,
Then what have we to do with Fascist Spain?

'Neutrality' has varying degrees;
Some states are so by enemy direction,
(Whom we so unaccountably appease,
While cool to those of unimpugned perfection
Who merely profit from the law by which
Belligerents grow poor and neutrals rich.)

Why with base Pétain are we moderate,
Steeped in the vileness of collaboration?
Why do we favour Franco's bloody state
Who first invited Nazi occupation?
It is not for the safety of the Rock,
But to cement a post-war Latin Bloc.

For in high places still vain hopes are nourished
A Franco-Spanish combine to contrive,
And with Rome too, where liberty once flourished,
But not the lees of freedom now survive,
Since her decline and fall without a stoppage
To the degraded level of the wop age.

At what expense of honour, gold and trouble
These hidden hands are working to restore
A quaking bastion of authentic rubble!
Their Latin Bloc is rotten to the core.
The world bears witness as the war proceeds,
Latins that fester smell far worse than Swedes.


## STERLING VALUES

It is important to base our actions on the prospect of a long war.
The decisive factor will be the maintenance of the spirit of the people
which depends on keeping a sound financial front. — Lord Kindersley,
September 18th, 1942.

If Britain hold fast
Till the war cloud has passed,
    Or adventure on desperate chances,
Our will to resist
Will only persist
    Through the soundness of British finances.

Essential supplies
Are obtained from Allies
  By means of beneficent barter,
So a huge foreign debt
Will not have to be met,
  As implied in the relevant Charter.


It is clear as the day
We are keeping at bay
  The spectre of money inflation,
Though notes may be printed
In billions unstinted
  Designed for home front circulation.


Our credit will stand
Every wartime demand
  If we husband our mighty resources,
But it could not sustain
A superfluous strain
  Like extravagant pay for the forces.


By management sound
Enough will be found
  For maximum all-out production,
But we cannot consent
Funds be borrowed or lent
  For reckless post-war reconstruction.


With savings secure,
We are steeled to endure,
  No matter how high we are tested,
And our fight for the free
Has the State guarantee
  That our earnings are safely invested.

Our standing financial
Is firm and substantial
    And our pace is unflagging, though leisurely,
While our pounds and our pence
Go in bonds for defence
    And our soul is laid up in the Treasury.


## STATE YOUTH
### [*After Lord Tennyson*]

The primary duty of national education is . . . to encourage in the individual an ardent understanding of the State's needs. The ideal of the nation as a leader among the nations . . . is the necessary first task of national education in the United Kingdom. — Interim Report of the Conservative Sub-Committee on Education, September 5th, 1942.

You must wake and call me early, call me early, mother, please,
If you do not rouse me promptly I shall never sleep at ease,
For to-morrow is the march-past of the Public School Brigade,
And I'm leading the Youth Day parade, mother, I'm leading the State
    Youth parade.

There'll be many a black, black eye, mother, if State Youth rises late,
For certain elements, they say, would trifle with the State,
And in this glad new year, mother, none may the call evade,
And I'm leading the Youth Day parade, mother, I'm leading the State
    Youth parade.

You know that Britain's youth, mother, by blood and birth and breed
Is called among the nations to guide and teach and lead;
In parts of all the earth, they say, our rule will be obeyed,
And I'm leading the Youth Day parade, mother, I'm leading the State
    Youth parade.

You never can have known, mother, the elemental thrill
Of spontaneous submission to the State's collective will;
But it is felt to-day, they say, in every social grade,
And I'm leading the Youth Day parade, mother, I'm leading the State
  Youth parade.

I cannot help but feel, mother, your youth was wild and weak
For you had no education in the national *mystique*,
In swamps of party politics your footsteps slipped and strayed,
But I'm leading the Youth Day parade, mother, I'm leading the State
  Youth parade.

I'll sleep so sound all night, mother, and dream that, marching by,
As I pass the flag-draped bandstand I shall catch our Leader's eye.
And you'll come with little Effie, who'll soon be a State Youth Maid,
For I'm leading the Youth Day parade, mother, I'm leading the State
  Youth parade.


## CROAKED THE EAGLE: 'NEVERMORE!'
### [*After Edgar Allan Poe*]

While the bombers, southward flocking, set Italian cities rocking,
Suddenly there came a knocking at Il Duce's office door.
He with fiery decision opened to admit a vision,
An expected apparition who had often called before —
  Destiny at hand once more.

Into that apartment regal slunk instead a Roman eagle,
Moping, moulting and bedraggled and extremely sick and sore,
With its plumage torn and tattered, beak and talons badly battered
And morale completely shattered, flapped and flopped upon the floor —
  Only that and nothing more.

'Answer!' cried the Fascist showman, 'emblem of the conquering Roman,
Fowl of Fate, and bird of omen, winging from the Libyan shore!
When shall my Imperial legions drive the Allies from those regions,
When shall I through Alexandria lead the Axis desert Korps?'
    Croaked the eagle 'Nevermore!'

'When will rebel Abyssinians yield up their usurped dominions?
When will Suez and Tunisia fall as spoils of glorious war?
When will Africa surrender to Islam's ordained defender?
When shall I sweep Mare Nostrum, undisputed conqueror?'
    Croaked the eagle 'Nevermore!'

'When with Fascist ceremonial entering my realms colonial,
Shall I reign from captive Hellas to the forfeited Côte d'Or?
When shall my resolve tenacious lead to conquests still more spacious,
When shall I Rome's world-wide empire of antiquity restore?'
    Croaked the eagle 'Definitely, positively, unequivocally,
      categorically, irretrievably, inexorably, irrevocably and
      finally — Nevermore!'

*November* 1942


## THE LAST PROCESSION

In a dozen countries Hitler's firing parties are at work every morning, and a dark stream of cold execution blood flows between the Germans and almost all their fellow-men. — The Prime Minister, September 8th, 1942

The Germans love processions; there will be
One more procession when the war is done,
That they may know what triumphs they have won
As the Third Reich advanced to victory.

The Germans love processions; they will stand
The whole day long to see their heroes come
With martial splendour and with beating drum,
Bringing new laurels for the Fatherland.

The crowning spectacle they shall not miss,
When subject peoples, vanquished in the war,
Crowd to pay homage to the conqueror
In sign of everlasting armistice.

Then from the north a coffined host will wind,
Norwegian villagers and fisher-folk,
At first ungrateful for the German yoke,
But afterwards to servitude resigned.

And from the west approaches will advance
A silent concourse bringing service due,
A punctual and subservient retinue,
The thousand butchered hostages of France.

And from the south, those who had made their peace
With the unconquerable German State,
The slaughtered youth of the Protectorate,
And men interred alive in Crete and Greece.

And from the east, a countless multitude
From mile-long barrows, for the buried rise,
Though earth were heaped upon their living eyes,
Slav bondsmen to their vassalage subdued.

And after them the children, laid on biers,
Like effigies of childhood carved in stone,
These infant foes on German mercy thrown,
Their claw-hands crossed, their grey cheeks stained with tears.

And last, returning to their capital,
Those Germans, suspect in the German cause,
Who were enlightened in the Third Reich laws,
And died unseen and had no burial.

The Germans love processions; they will see
Along their streets, beneath their windows drawn,
Through nights and days and many a steely dawn,
That last procession pass the Chancellery.

So still, so silent will the conquered come,
Where once in triumph German legions came,
So death will cry aloud the German name,
Bringing the harvest of the Third Reich home.


## FORGOTTEN MEN

'The authorities who shut up these men for their hostility to the Axis
Powers are to determine whether and when they are released. . . . Mr.
Eden . . . could give no answer about International Brigade prisoners.'
— *Manchester Guardian*, November 27th, 1942.

There was an International Brigade
Which fought for freedom with foolhardy passion,
Before the International Crusade
Became the fashion.

Their hopeless fight they fought out to the end,
Their wounds and scars their only decorations;
When they stood fast their statesmen did not send
Congratulations.

They did not die to save their native state,
Some, liberty's exiles, no State possessing,
They bled for an ideal but did not wait
The Church's blessing.

Their victories were not their nation's boast,
No war memorials inscroll their glory,
Spain's tragedy and theirs, is an almost
Forgotten story.

Forgotten, like the men now left to rot,
While freedom's champions treat with Spain's Dictator,
And raise to power the Vichy patriot,
A double traitor.

Because they fought too soon in freedom's war,
Though grave their fault, their fate deserves compassion —
Men should not fight for liberty before
It is the fashion.


## GENIUS FOR UNDERSTATEMENT
[*After Lord Macaulay*]

Now glory to our great Ally in her triumphant hour!
And glory to her C.-in-C., tall General Eisenhower!
Indomitable is the force he landed from the sea,
And south he strikes to Mogador and east to Tripoli!
False Darlan has surrendered; Algiers is in his hands,
The Bey of Tunis, trembling, submits to his commands.
De Gaulle has called the Fighting French to swell the grand advance,
And save from traitor hirelings the pleasant land of France!
Hurrah for General Eisenhower and Général Giraud!
(And, by the way, the British Fleet is putting up a show.)

Hurrah for the Red Army that stood at Moscow's gate,
And drove the mighty Wehrmacht back with all its armoured weight!
Twice have the Panzer spearheads thrust, and twice been held at bay,
Oh, never in the tale of war was such a bloody fray!
Now Stalingrad's defenders stand, now the invader falls,
And cold and stiff and stark they lie beneath her blackened walls.
The army that was hurled against the ramparts of the east
Across the vast and icy steppes crawls like a wounded beast.
Now General Winter takes the field, the Russian wolf-packs hunt.
(And, by the way, the British have pulled off a second front.)

Now God be thanked for China and for gallant Chiang Kai-shek!
Right well he led the five-year fight to keep the foe in check!
A hundred times the Japanese seemed closing in a ring,
A hundred times fell back before the onslaught from Chungking!
Our Allies, Free Chinese stand firm against the ruthless foe
And fling back their defiance to the war-lords of Tokyo!
And now the Japs are driven from their bases in Chekiang
Bursts from the line a deafening shout, 'Give praise for General Chiang!
The enemy is in retreat!  Pursue him as he flies!'
(And, by the way, the R.A.F. is cleaning up the skies.)

Ho! maidens of Vienna; ho! matrons of Berlin,
Reich victory, so long proclaimed, is but a might-have-been.
Weep, weep and rend your hair for those who will return no more,
For Russians and Americans have turned the tide of war!
Ho! leaders of the Axis hordes, your forces are in flight!
Ho! craven lord of Italy, keep watch and ward to-night!
Trapped Rommel in the desert flees before his broken ranks,
The sands are heaped with guns and gear, crashed planes and burnt-
    out tanks.
The captured forts of Libya haul down the German flag.
(And, by the way, Montgomery has Rommel in the bag.)

*November* 1942

# EDEN'S FAREWELL TO DE GAULLE

*[After 'The Arab's Farewell to his Steed']*

It was intended ... De Gaulle should broadcast to Europe. The script was submitted for approval ... and approved by Mr. Eden ... subsequently it was suppressed. — Mr. Stokes, M.P., November 24th, 1942.

Mon Général! mon Général! who standest fiercely by,
With thy fiery but unuttered speech, and dark accusing eye,
Fret not to roam the desert now with thine impetuous speed,
Another voice is raised for France, her fighting force to lead —
Thou shalt not scour the distant plain to rally French morale,
There is no reasonable doubt, thou'rt sold, mon Général!
Arrangements of our great Ally are not to be controlled;
Another steals thy thunder now, mon Général! thou'rt sold.

And shall I follow Washington and back Darlan's cabal?
I may not take thy side again; farewell! mon Général!
Farewell! farewell! and yet, may not a formula be found?
Whatever Darlan may proclaim, it seems we are not bound;
And dost thou think mine ancient pledge was merest persiflage,
And is thy dream of Fighting France naught now but false mirage?
Ah! when I hear another call to rouse the Arab Sheik,
How sadly I'll recall the time when last I let thee speak!

When last I let thee speak? Away! the fever'd dream is o'er,
That ill-considered censorship shall part us twain no more.
They tempted me, mon Général! with hopes of compromise,
The moment French North Africa declared for the Allies.
Who said that I had giv'n thee up, who said that thou wert sold?
'Tis false, 'tis false, mon Général! I shall, like thee, be bold!
They tempted me to turn thee down — but no, it cannot be —
Though thou wert sold, mon Général! thou wast not sold by me.

# NO FLIES

It is not surprising that the (Darlan) situation should be regarded here with dismay as well as disgust ... it has disheartened the lesser Allies who ask if Quislings everywhere are to be accorded most-favoured-traitor treatment. — *Spectator*.

'Will you walk into my parlour?' said the spider to the fly,
'In the common cause of freedom I can use a new ally,
The way into my parlour is up a private stair,
And we'll not be interrupted while we settle our affair.'

So Vichy's boneless wonder with Eisenhower conferred
In a snug Algerian parlour where they were not overheard,
And the spider and the fly agreed upon a joint design
And both affixed their signatures upon the dotted line.

So the Austrian ex-archduke sought out Secretary Hull,
For a war is not the moment for a diplomatic lull,
And Foreign Office parlours made their preparations too
When Hungarians and Slovaks asked a quiet interview.

When diplomatic spiders span their snares of ancient shape
According to the oft-told tale, the fly could not escape,
The unsuspecting visitor was always overpowered,
There were no flies on the spider and the insect was devoured.

But the quisling fly is unexcelled at skirting round the web
While the giant spider's *savoir faire* has reached its lowest ebb,
For, far from being swallowed in the spider's artful grip,
The fly is seen departing with a junior spider-ship.

So United Nation spinners give concern to small Allies,
Though their parlours are wide open and they simply crawl with flies.
Each fly may be the tenant of a comfortable niche —
There are flies and there are spiders — but God knows which is which.

# THE LAST ALL CLEAR

On some grey morning after hideous night,
There'll be an end of terror and listening fear,
When shelterers and the watchers on the height
Will catch the note of the siren, steady and swelling,
The single, strident call of the last all clear,
Over the empty street and the darkened dwelling.

Then sleepers will start upright at the sound,
The black cloths suddenly from the windows torn,
And none that day will tread the common ground.
We'll walk on air, and know transfiguration,
And see familiar things like souls new born
Upon the earliest morning of creation.

There'll be such high commotion in that dim
Day-break, such cockcrow clamour at sunrise,
Trumpets of everlasting cherubim,
Skylarks and clarions at the gates of heaven,
That everyone will hear without surprise
When news of peace is broadcast at eleven.

One spellbound morning, after months or years,
Startling the cloudy darkness it will come
With singing stars, with music of the spheres,
With lost bells clashing from the scarecrow towers.
That age, that moment of millennium,
Let come what may, will certainly be ours.

1935 — 40

## THE VOICE THAT BREATHED O'ER EDEN
### OR
### THE GENIUS OF GENEVA

I spray cool showers on the heated Powers,
In international scenes,
Ease strained relations between Croatians
And hot-on-the-scent Slovenes.
I soothe alarms raised by States-in-arms
And, saved from their own supporters,
I keep the Slavs, already in halves,
From carving themselves in quarters.

I play the shepherd to wolf and leopard,
I fondle the lion's paws,
And show the eagle it's quite illegal
To rend the lamb in its claws.
Through me the weak can vent their pique,
(And never the strong yelled louder)
With joy extreme they can let off steam
So long as they save the powder.

Though bloodstained Japs may quit perhaps,
And the Teutons are simply appalling,
I call them still, like the lost Brazil,
And shall to the end be calling.
I waft my orders to distant borders
At the boom of the first attack,
Their ways to soften, though all too often
My orders are wafted back.

My voice delivers the world from rivers,
And possibly seas, of blood,
I blunt each blow at the *status quo*
And therefore my name is mud.
Each new alliance may shout defiance
And tension each day increase,
Whoever pleases may keep the pieces
So long as I keep the peace.


## ULTIMATUM TO PEACE

Dove of the world's desire,
Hymned by the nations' choir,
Wilt thou to Heaven retire,
Deaf to discussion?
Cold to the Powers' whole
Plan for armed peace control?
Canst thou not hear the Pole?
Know'st thou not Russian?

Soarest thou out of reach
Even of English speech?
Can France's peace-time screech
Fail to allure thee?
Is then thy German scant
Balked by the Nazi's cant?
Or does Il Duce's rant
Not reassure thee?

Read'st thou not guarantees
Given in Japanese?
Can such transparent pleas,
Goddess, unnerve thee?

States, dropping warfare crass,
Arms for thy sake amass,
Say it with poison gas,
But to preserve thee!

Over thine empty chair
Damocles' sword in air
Hangs by a single hair,
Ready to fall now.
Come on thy silver wing,
Come with a piece of string,
Tie up the dangling thing
Once and for all now!

Goddess or bird obtuse,
Thee will no pact induce?
Hast for this bristling truce
Small predilection?
Then nothing less than war,
Peace, will thy reign restore.
Slain must thou be before
Thy resurrection!


## THE HARDENED BRAT

I met a little cottage brat,
Her petticoat was red.
She had some contradiction flat
For everything I said.

I took the tombstone next to her,
She gave a dirty grin,
And stirred her little porringer
That had no porridge in.

I told her that I had been sent
To teach the unemployed
The blessings of this Government . . .
She only seemed annoyed.

I said: 'We keep food prices high
And subsidize the land,
Lest it should chance the food supply
Might equal the demand.'

Of levies on imported meat
I then began to speak.
She said: 'We live and dress and eat
On one pound eight per week.'

I asked: 'How many may you be
That gratis we maintain?'
She answered: 'Ma and Pa and me,
Since we lost John and Jane.'

Our recent budgetary gain
I next enlarged upon.
She said: 'You're sitting down on Jane,
I'm sitting down on John.'

I said: 'Our records we affix
To hoardings in the town.'
She said: 'John died at three-and-six
And Jane at half-a-crown.'

I praised our charity about
The means test and the cuts.
She said: 'Young John and Jane passed out
Because they'd got no guts.'

'And furthermore, till Pa is dead,
He'll never get a job.
But if I die for it,' she said,
'I'll live to fifteen bob!'

I left the tombstone next to her,
She gave a dirty grin,
And stirred her little porringer
That had no porridge in.


# FEE, FI, FO, FUM!

When Ethiopians roar to unleash the dogs of war,
And sharpen savage knives,
When woolly-haired slave-traders dare call noble Romans raiders
They must answer with their lives.
I was born to put in place this swarthy subject race
Whose conquest fires my veins,
To swot the Abyssinians as old Rome the Carthaginians,
And I am only waiting for the rains.

We Romans need not blench when supported by the French,
By Belgium, Spain and Greece,
While Jugo-Slav and Czecho- both applaud us to the echo
And Britain whimpers 'Peace!'
Imperial states provide war sinews for my side,
Free transit for my planes,
And Suez welcomes shipment of my debited equipment,
And I am only waiting for the rains.

Our Fascist cause is just but we like our rivals trussed,
So the Powers at my back
Safeguard my expedition by withholding ammunition
From the base and menial black.
Though our treaties are not kept that we drafted while we slept
No blot our honour stains,
For we understand each other and the black is *not* our brother,
And I am only waiting for the rains.

Let the Ethiope intrigue with the lily-livered League,
The League his grievance air;
By the Ides of this September I'll no longer be a member,
And he will not be there.
No force shall me despoil of Abyssinia's soil!
On conquering campaigns
I am Caesar and Sejanus, Mussolini Africanus!
Advance! I am not waiting for the rains.


## HOW THEY BROUGHT THE BAD NEWS
## FROM GENEVA TO ADDIS ABABA

'We might even see the spectacle of Italy carrying out a punitive
expedition into Abyssinia with the apparent approval of the League.' —
'Critic', on the work of the Committee of Five in the *New Statesman
and Nation*, Sept. 14th.

They sprang into action a peace to contrive;
The Council, the League, the Committee of Five;
'Good speed!' cried the Parties of pacifist views;
'Speed!' echoed the members with nothing to lose;
The Assembly applauded goodwill to attest,
As they scourged the aggressor and soothed the aggressed.

The League of all Nations in lofty debate
Foretold Abyssinia saved from her fate,
They shuddered and shrank at the rumour of war,
For they loved empire well but the Covenant more,
While the victim proposed they might well intervene
Under Articles 20 or 10 or 16.

While Laval looked to Hoare and Hoare looked to Laval
To sanction joint Sanctions or shut the Canal,
While the Five with acute international tact
Offered protocol, treaty, agreement or pact,
And ministers ended preambles sublime
With 'Let us do nothing while yet there is time!'

Up leaped then at Addis Ababa the sun!
The States from commitments drew back every one.
Each eyeing his nearest next neighbour askance
In the shock and surprise of the Fascist advance,
And the Negus, bamboozled, marched down to receive a
Report from Il Duce on News from Geneva.


## GUERRA BELLISSIMA!

'War is beautiful when it fills the flowering meadow with the flaming orchids of grapeshot . . . when it makes a symphony of guns and cannon-shots . . . songs of soldiers, odours of putrefaction.' — *Gazzetta del Popolo*.

> *Guerra bellissima*
> Fascist-envisaged!
> Bone taut and vibrant
> Hums with the bullet!
> Flesh juvenescent
> Leaps to the missile's
> Kiss metallurgic!

Wounds of carnation
Gushing warm purple
Effluent viscera,
Red vermicelli,
Glazed, gleaming eyeballs,
Sparking, viridian,
Clay phosphorescent
Rank in corruption,
Burn on Mars' palette
Loved hues of carnage!

Pale putrefaction,
Bone unresponsive,
Flesh gashed in half-tones,
Pallid intestines,
Death-stench insipid,
Mark war's cold carrion
Void of Fascismo!

Iron-tongued loud-speakers
Boost neo-Roman
Art morticultural!
Beat on the ear-drums,
Bark in the city,
Bawl in the mountains,
Blast in the valleys,
Boom in the jungle,
Bray in the desert
Rapture aesthetic,
War's apotheosis,
Fascist boloney!

'The time for some step to be taken could not be fixed now . . . the Government were, however, not unaware of the importance of the matter, and preliminary examination of the problem had now been begun.' — Vicount Cranborne in reply to question in House of Commons, Feb. 5th, on Economic Conference, or, more briefly, Government answer to almost anything.

'We, who the course of England keep,
we hold it true whate'er befall,
look long enough, you need not leap
at all.
We weigh the pro against the con,
count consequence on consequence,
perched imperturbably upon
the fence.
Green governments in fragments fly
by breakneck action undermined;
strong words pass by us like the i-
dle wind.
Encrusted on the ship of state
perpetual barnacles are we,
they longest serve who only wait
and see.'

# CLEAR AS MUD

'Mandated territories are not colonies ... they are only part of the British Empire in what I may call a colloquial sense.' — Neville Chamberlain, House, April 8th.

'Colonies are colonies,' said the Chancellor,
The dark horizon cleared.
'Mandates are mandates,' said the Chancellor,
The Commons rose and cheered.
There's not a palm or a fellah,
Kopje or wallah or crag,
But is for ever the Empire
When once it is under the flag.

*But mandates may fly to the Nazis*
*As soon as the League allows,*
*And the Cameroons long for the Nazis*
*As the spinster longs for a spouse.*

'Colonies are not mandates,' said the Chancellor,
'They shall not be transferred.
'Mandates are not colonies,' said the Chancellor,
'Whoever said so, erred.'
Let the Nazis possess Tanganyika,
That an era of peace may begin,
Tanganyika pants after the Nazis
As the butterfly pants for the pin.

*Samoa is athirst for the Nazis*
*As thirsts for Fascismo the Ras,*
*And Togoland turns to the Nazis*
*As the suicide turns to the gas.*

'*Romeo and Juliet* . . . is said to have been of great assistance to the current campaign on behalf of family life.' — Moscow News Item.

The rationale of these events,
when we collate and analyse
their sociologic elements,
viz.: Montague *v.* Capulet,
show sacredness of kindred ties.
The aged Boyar in his halls
marked down a mate for Juliet,
his family and offspring sole
(though he for that was not to blame,
his lady practised birth-control).
But then in disobedience wild
the aforementioned Juliet came,
with Romeo, her Montague,
to die before she had a child
to join Verona's daily brawls,
continuing the collective feud
where Capulets and Montagues,
in some remote relation's cause,
ran one another through and through.
This cousinhood did not exclude
far-distant uncles and in-laws,
but kin to kindred stuck like glue,
and none, though sentenced, would consent
to waste good feuds in banishment.

How different are conditions here
where comrade-fathers slip the bond,
abandoning relations near,
raise progeny in various spots
and irresponsibly abscond,

bequeathing the paternal State
full custody of wife and tots.
(An absentee Odessa Dad
lightly begets in Leningrad,
and ere his wife can say My God!
decamps to Nijni Novgorod.)

Such comrades should assimilate
the lesson of this tragedy
with social implications plain
in praise of consanguinity,
and promiscuity discard.
The Soviet State could then maintain
that blackguard Britain's bourgeois Bard
had lived not utterly in vain.

---

## LOCARNO

*Talks — 9 a.m. to 3 a.m.*                    *R.S.V.P.*

---

'It is excellent that the Government have succeeded in their efforts to
bring both Germany and Italy to a new Locarno Conference.' — *The
Times*, Aug. 6th.

Great Britain in the nick again has turned the saving trick again
With diplomatic brilliance famed in Foreign Office feats;
Five peace-pledged Powers are able now to bargain round a table now
Where everybody shows his hand, and everybody cheats.

The Gallic and Britannic Powers, the Roman and Germanic Powers,
Trustees of peace, and bodyguard to Flander's pocket State,
Will swap impressive homilies on regional anomalies
And cry for sacred treaties which are truly up-to-date.

Democracy's vicissitude claims democrats' solicitude,
But claims are out of order while new compromises pend;
The French their Social labours crown by letting Spanish neighbours
     down,
Dictators are so coy to catch, so fatal to offend!

The British, quite invincible in all affairs of principle,
Forestalling an occurrence which already has occurred,
Present the torn Peninsula a front superbly insular,
Their rôle as freedom's champion expediently deferred!

With pandering persuasiveness pursuing shrewd evasiveness
Lawbreakers are solicited as guardians of the law;
Fascisti must be mollified and Nazis not disqualified
So that the Men of Destiny may lead the men of straw.

So Belgium with full weight again they'll swear inviolate again
And mutually ratify their rock-ribbed guarantees,
When war's eventuality makes hay of her neutrality,
She'll count on hospitality for future refugees.

Now sternly warning Nemesis from Governmental premises
The European Concert reads its complicated score
With aptitude professional rehearsing their Recessional
The Stresa Three will harmonize with the Locarno Four.

Though heading for futurity in chronic insecurity,
The European system holds precariously intact,
But plighted cunning mending it can only end by ending it . . .
We might survive another War but not another Pact.

'Germany's currency is stable and in no circumstances will be devalued.' — Ministry of Finance.

'Germany has, of course, virtually no gold or gold exchange reserve.' — *Manchester Guardian*, Sept. 29th.

> A State defaults on foreign debts,
> It goes its happy, bankrupt way,
> And astronomic credit gets
> Because it does not mean to pay.
>
> The solvent States, to ease the strain,
> Devaluate before a fall,
> Till none at last on gold remain
> But States that have no gold at all.

## LEST WE FORGET

'I wonder whether, for the League's sake and our own, we ought not to give formal notice now that we propose to leave it.' — A. P. Herbert, *Standard*, Oct. 5th.

'We submit ourselves whole-heartedly, nay gladly, to the Covenant of the League of Nations.' — Winston Churchill, Sept. 24th.

> Ways of our fathers, known of yore,
> Who bagged the earth by right divine,
> And beaconed lesser breeds before
> The League arose to our design,
> Self-interest plus self-righteousness
> No longer seems a great success.

The Island Race, the Nelson touch,
The word-more-binding-than-the-bond
Do not appear to count for much,
The lesser breeds do not respond,
And none our services engage
In tasks of honest brokerage.

The lesser breeds, not in our care,
Who hailed the League with hope renewed
Imply that we their evils bear
With far too noble fortitude,
While at Geneva nothing's heard
But Eden breaking Baldwin's word.

Now, while we still equivocate,
And neither lead nor leave alone,
Should we not quit the doomed debate
Lest the League's cause become our own?
And with our Fascist friends depart
Lest we might make a fairer start?

Lest we reverse the rôle antique
We inauspiciously prolong
Of always pleading with the weak
While always siding with the strong,
Lest we forget, lest we forget,
And make good Europeans yet?

# VOX ROMANORUM

'Signor Mussolini was presented with the Sword of Islam . . . at a ceremony near Tripoli . . . in the name of the soldiers and Moslems of Libya. Addressing the crowd Signor Mussolini emphasized his words by waving his sword in the air.' — *The Times*, March 19th, 1937.

Say, listen, Libya!
This is Babe Benito First, Second, Fifth and Tenth!
Vittorio Emanuele the Third,
He's the band on my cigar.
Wotthehell, I made him Emp'ror, ain't I?
He ain't got no kick coming.
Sure Abyssinia's a bunch of lousy niggers,
But the goddam British Empire ain't nothin' else.
Maybe I take it, one day.
I'm Babe Benito!

Get this, Geneva!
I guess I told you where you get off.
I guess I'm boss all right.
Maybe you remember Abyssinia. . . .
Laff that off, you bastards!
Get this, you non-intervention sissies,
I'm givin' the Reds the bum's rush outta Spain.
I bet Madrid's a second Addis Ababa
Before you can say Caesar!

I'm Babe Benito.
I ain't no Hitler, handin' out five-cent pledges,
To one-horse States, crazy to make the headlines,
Gassing to yes-men in a lousy Opera House.
I tell the world from a tractor, a cannon, a war-horse;
They take it an' like it.

Hell, I got England scared silly, ain't I?
I'll say I got the drop on Vienna!
I'll say the Lion of Judah's a laff all right!
I'll say I got the Vatican where I want it!
Jeese, an' now I'm Defender of Islam.


Listen, Libya!
I'm Defender of Islam all right.
I don't need no goddam son of a mullah to gimme the o.k.
Maybe you seen me give the Rases the works!
An' if there's any funny business you know what's coming
    to you.
I'm Babe Benito.



## THE DRESS REHEARSAL

The Spaniard's blood is fiery, the Spaniard's head is hot,
The Spaniards' quarrels are their own, the Spanish War is not;
As amateurs they flew to arms, not even knowing how,
And, lacking expert aid, the scrap would be all over now.


But war-trained Powers took the field with small hope of reward,
To save the modern world the shame of fighting with the sword,
They lavished field-equipment and the necessary men,
For just a little looting and some plunder now and then.


They shelled, and they bombarded, and they mechanized the ranks
With armoured-cars, machine-guns, and artillery and tanks,
They filled the sky with bombers and they strewed the sea with mines
And mowed militia down with guns of intricate designs.

So when all volunteers were by non-intervention banned,
They had to send out armies and assume the high command,
And the hundred-thousand Fascists who now animate the scene
Are naturally hostile when the Spaniards intervene.

While sharing full expenses in the observation posts
To make all neutral ships 'move on' around the Spanish coasts,
Their expeditionary force involves a double cost,
But they know the opportunity too precious to be lost.

The seven-and-twenty nations who agree to stand apart
From this striking demonstration of the military art,
Combine to make these critical manœuvres a success,
Whatever other sentiments their citizens profess.

In Spain the newest theories of the Staffs can be applied,
In Spain they test inventions, never previously tried,
For Spain's the dress-rehearsal, with effects not seen before,
For the final presentation on a world-wide scene of war.

## PAJAROS NEGROS[1]

'A hideous week in Spain has involved the complete destruction of Guernica ... little doubt remains that it was the exclusive work of German aeroplanes and bombers.' — *Observer*, May 2nd.

Black birds over Guernica roaring and wheeling,
fighters and bombers hawking and swooping in chase
over the tottering churches, the farmsteads, the reeling
houses and market-place,

[1] Pájaros négros (black birds), the current Spanish phrase for the great Junker bombers.—*The Times*, April 30th.

filling the eyes with the image of terror, and filling
the ears with the screams of the buried under the walls,
droning and drumming, soaring and zooming, rending and killing,
glutted as darkness falls.

Leaving the place of their feasting blackened and burning,
leaving the ruins for omen, the dead for a sign,
black birds voided of death to their eyries returning
honoured over the Rhine.

Who shall avenge Guernica? None will avenge her,
It is not the blood of our children that cries from the ground.
Death has no summons to call from the sky the revenger,
the murdered make no sound.

Over our shifts and surrenders, connivance unending,
hover the smoke and the reek of that smouldering pyre.
We will remember Guernica when black birds descending
*our* cities set on fire.


## WOOSTER OF WHITEHALL

[*With apologies to P. G. Wodehouse*]

Well chappies, here we are, smoothing out the old fracas,
We've got control and all that sort of rot.
I've explored the whole posish, but I won't cry stinking fish,
Or the thing would absolutely go to pot.

I exude the good old tact *re* the breaches of the pact,
And I've beetled in to pour the spot of oil,
For the world feels safe and sound if we Woosters rally round
While the dear old League is pro tem. off the boil.

I maintain the cool perspective on the jolly old objective,
Prolonged pourparlers are my cup of tea;
Though I mop the streaming brow when the colleagues start a row,
For we only meet to beat about the b.

Old Franco understands he may use whatever lands
So long as no one gives away the show;
But I get the bally pip and the thing eludes the grip
When some blisters go and publish all they know.

When I see the heavy fist I am swift to grasp the gist
(We Woosters aren't the copper on the beat).
If at night we hurl the warning, we withdraw it in the morning
And jolly well remove the British Fleet.

We'll remain the old school friend till the bust up's at an end,
And Valencia's mangled fragments are inhaled;
Then you'll all feel pretty braced that no step was stepped in haste,
And a cordial cameraderie prevailed.

We perceive the snag that lurks in the present painful circs.,
As we referee the doings from afar;
And the strength for holding back while we take the dirty crack,
Is the thing that makes us Woosters what we are.


## NO FLOWERS

### League of Nations Assembly. May, 1937

'Say not the struggle naught availeth!'
We still discuss the status quo.
Geneva's radiant sunrise paleth,
There lingers yet the afterglow.

And none the less the world advances
Piecemeal towards our peaceful goal
Though we perceive when circumstances
Have passed beyond the League's control.

Though there be reason for dejection
In Abyssinia, Danzig, Spain,
Such instances of imperfection
Are lessons never learned in vain.

Freed from the idealist's confusion
We hold the realistic view,
And banning sanctions and exclusion,
A broader Covenant renew.

No more impatient of fruition,
Each painful setback we survive,
More constant in decomposition
Than when we thought we were alive.

## COMPLETE AMUSEMENT GUIDE

SUNDAY.

Great Britain sews up Spain's *cordon sanitaire*,
French banks break the back of the *Front Populaire*,
The Rome-Berlin Axis puts states in a spin,
And the Little Entente is uneasy within.

MONDAY.

Schacht showers on Danubia the boon of Reich trade,
Von Neurath is voted *de trop* in Belgrade,
The *Queen Mary* leaves dry-dock as Queen of the Sea,
And U.S.A. strikers are making whoopee.

TUESDAY.

The Little Entente shares identical views,
Spain's naval patrols are transferred to canoes,
Japan with acclaim joins the peacemaker's ring,
And Cathleen na Hooligan blows up a King.

WEDNESDAY.

Great Britain's prosperity booms at the peak,
The Chancellor cancels the tax of the week,
Half the Little Entente gives the Nazi salute,
And citizen Stalin is off on a shoot.

THURSDAY.

The Windsors are offered the Austrian crown,
Geneva breaks up, and world trade-talks break down,
The Duce earns Hitler's *ur-nordische* badge,
And Congress in India gives the razz to the Raj.

FRIDAY.

The charm of Ciano disarms Budapest,
Newspapers all over the world are suppressed,
The Balkans dissolve and announce a fresh start,
And the Little Entente keeps on falling apart.

SATURDAY.

Esthonia plans to become self-contained,
Reich sovereignty over all *Wurst* is regained,
The Solomon Islands make ready for war —
And the Little Entente is the same as before.

# CULTURAL ATTACHÉS

OR

# INTELLIGENT ANTICIPATION

'There is a proposal that "cultural attachés" should be appointed to the more important embassies . . . (it is clearly the desire of the [Nazi] Party leaders that they should be accorded full diplomatic privileges); and it is proposed that London should have the honour of being the first country to receive these additional members of the *corps diplomatique*.' — *The Times*, Aug. 31st.

If you wake at midnight and hear a stifled scream,
It is probably a German getting wise to the *régime*;
Don't go calling the police or make excited sounds,
It's the cultural attachés on their diplomatic rounds.

Cultural attachés,
Snooping after dark,
Sniffing round St. James's,
Snuffing round the Park,
Prying at the key-hole,
Sidling out and in,
All for making London a suburb of Berlin.

Nazi culture shock-troops, trained in manly games,
Spouting Nazi values, touting Nazi claims,
Keeping close surveillance with superior technique
While sheltered in the bosom of the *corps diplomatique*.

Twenty thousand Germans somewhat out of hand,
Nazi ideology will shortly understand,
While Anglo-Nazi fellowships facilities arrange
For ethico=political-aesthetical exchange.

230

Renegades and refugees taken by surprise,
England as a breeding ground for little Nazi spies,
If these cultural activities raise question or demur
A diplomatic cleavage will infallibly occur.

Ferrets of the Third Reich,
Spreading mystic urge,
Here and there a pogrom,
Now and then a purge;
If you see a body
Don't go butting in,
Just get used to London as a suburb of Berlin.


## UNFOUNDED RUMOURS

'There have been rumours recently that some action by the Assembly of the League of Nations is contemplated with a view to "regularising" the position of Italy in Abyssinia ... we may be confident that our Government will not be guilty of such a betrayal of international law and justice.' — Letter from Dr. Gilbert Murray and Lord Cecil. *The Times*, Aug. 24th.

We will banish groundless rumours from men's hearing,
Which refutations only seem to spread,
We will resurrect the faith, fast disappearing,
That Britain always means what she has said,
We will steadily and mightily revive
The great Hoare pledge of 1935.
We will not yield to bluster or defiance,
Or give Imperial Fascist claims support,
To purchase by perfidious compliance
Mediterranean peace, however short.

Above intrigues and sophistries Genevan,
The bargaining, the bleating and the blah,
When all the birds come home to roost at even
And hoot the knell of Abyssinia,
Unshaken on our unilateral course
We will condemn the fruits of lawless force.
Recovering her voice among the nations,
Great Britain, trumpet-tongued, will leave no doubt
That all these tales are baseless fabrications. . . .

It's curious how such rumours get about.


## ACROSS THE PYRENEES

'Downing St. is well aware that Franco has three fully-equipped Italian divisions of 80,000 men.' — Daily Papers, Oct. 19th.

O Eden, go and call the volunteers,
And call the volunteers
Across the Pyrenees,
Till lawless intervention disappears
On land as on the seas.

The chairman's sub-committee perseveres,
Invasion perseveres,
The Plymouth Brethren pray;
The sub-committee's sub-committee clears
Last obstacles away.

And every State to every plan adheres,
In principle adheres
To formulas worn thin,
While no impetuous action interferes
With Franco's scheduled win.

But when the picked Italian troops with cheers
Advance, with martial cheers,
With battle-airs and drums,
When, somehow leaking through Spain's shut frontiers,
The Fascist army comes,

With clang of armoured columns in men's ears,
(In all but Eden's ears)
It seems, in view of these,
Superfluous to call the volunteers
Across the Pyrenees.

## THE NEW LEAGUE

Rome's tripartite agreement shows
a white-hot coalescence;
its whole dynamic message glows
with Fascist incandescence.
Far, far beyond Geneva's reach,
pedantically legal,
this soaring and exultant screech
proclaims the Fascist eagle.

They hail the coming Fascist age
from Reich and Roman rostrum,
as now for Colonies they rage,
and now for Mare Nostrum!
And when they've purged from every land
Bolshevik desperadoes
the earth will be the Duce's (and
the Reich's and the Mikado's).

Above Geneva's stark remains
the Fascists turn the tables
and hurl totalitarian Cains
on democratic Abels,
while peace-pledged nations view with dread
their logical successor,
the new League of the anti-red
against the non-aggressor.


# PIRATE INTO PORPOISE

## [A Ballad of the Fleet]

'An official Admiralty statement says: It has been established that an attack on H.M.S. *Basilisk* was not made. An Admiralty official, commenting, said: We cannot tell what it was that appeared to be a torpedo. It might have been a porpoise, but we cannot really say.' — *News Chronicle*, Oct. 9th.

It was H.M.S. *Basilisk* patrolled the Spanish sea,
With the *Bluebottle* to windward and the *Bunfight* on her lee,
It was two bells in the forenoon, and no pirates to be seen,
When her submarine-detector twigged a skulking submarine.

They dusted off a depth-charge and allowed it time to drop,
They waited till an oily patch had risen to the top,
Then they signalled that the submarine had sunk with every soul,
And steamed off to join the *Bunfight* on the piracy patrol.

But Admiralty officials, being honourably bound
By a gentleman's agreement that no pirates should be found,
After full investigation when all evidence was weighed,
Announced a submarine attack was never really made.

The unconfirmed impression of the captain and the crew
Was ruled right out of hearing, as it plainly would not do,
But a chatty spokesman added to their terse communiqué,
'It might have been a porpoise, but we cannot really say.'

The oily patch was stated, after weeks of expert toil,
Consistent with a porpoise which had taken castor oil,
So the *Basilisk's* Commander, though he hadn't thought of that,
Said it might have been a porpoise that mistook her for a sprat.


QUID PRO NIL

More valiant and high-stepping Powers
Make war and glory their concern;
Shopkeeping nations such as ours
Invest against a safe return,
But business caution we suspend
To buy the Duce for a friend.

The price of his esteemed goodwill
(Without security) includes
The cost of Abyssinia's bill,
A loan advanced on stolen goods
Our shopsoiled honour goes as well
To purchase — what he has to sell.

Resolved to stick at no expense
To set aggression on its feet
We bribe with simple confidence
This bankrupt and unquestioned cheat
Who, once assisted to the top,
Will scheme to make us shut up shop.

Well-met above the corpse of Spain,
Extended credits we arrange,
The Duce basks in golden rain,
We keep Geneva — and the change.
The price we stoop to pay is high,
But what in God's name do we buy?


# HUMANITARIAN

As Franco's high explosives rain
From Barcelona's falling skies,
The Premier, recklessly humane,
Expostulates with his allies.

The world his pious horror hears,
But for that overflowing grave
It falls unheard on murdered ears
And mocks the dead he feared to save.


# ELEGY

*[After Oliver Goldsmith]*

'Great Britain makes a difficult sacrifice of principle by promising
to bring the question of the recognition of the sovereignty of Ethiopia
before the League of Nations.' — *The Times*, April 18th.

Good people all of every kind,
Unto my song give ear,
Of how the nations late combined
To make aggressors fear,

Of eight-and-fifty sheep-dogs, bound
No more to bark or bite,
And tainted wethers to impound
With full collective might.

A wolf in sheepskin was disclosed,
A lurking beast of prey.
The League his brigandage opposed,
*A mouton enragé* —

And more in sorrow than in ire
Put on the sanctions screw
To make the peacebreaker retire,
As they were sworn to do.

The killer ravaged, undismayed
By their coercive thrust,
The justice of his force outweighed
The forces of the just.

Their logic was confounded quite
As fact with theory vied,
The wolf recovered from the bite;
The League it was that died.


## THE GAME

Contestants for historic fame
Amid the European stress,
Benes and Hitler play their game
Of chess.

World experts keep the moves in view,
The pawns and pieces stand in line,
The Nazis call on Benes to
Resign.

Defeat beforehand to accept —
Like Schuschnigg, with a fool's-mate floored
When Austria moved and Hitler swept
The board.

Great Britain with smooth-tongued advice,
Assiduous to non-intervene,
Prescribes that Benes sacrifice
His Queen.

The French enjoin resistance stout,
Defence against the Nazi snatch,
No handicap, and playing out
The match.

Magyars, Rumanians and Poles
Wait for the Benes line to break.
Benes with fifteen million souls
At stake

Plays the Sudeten gambit first,
Manœuvring to save the State,
To force a draw and foil the worst —
Czechmate.

# PAINTING THE LILY

'Herr Hitler . . . could not believe it impossible to prevent the Press in democratic countries from printing "lies and calumnies".' — *Daily Telegraph*, March 12th.

You cannot paint the lily, nor
The violet perfume,
You cannot gild a golden ore
Nor blacken midnight gloom;
The honour of the Reich no less
Can be disparaged by the Press.

For credit rests on no report
And deeds themselves explain,
No journal can the facts distort
Of Austria and Spain,
The most tendentious versions pale
Before that true unvarnished tale.

The Reich which arts and science learns
By light from Streicher's lamp;
The Reich where a Niemöller earns
A concentration camp,
To all the world appears to be
Beyond the reach of calumny.

You cannot paint the lily, nor
Perfume the violet,
The records of the Reich outsoar
Newspaper epithet.
The Nazi State may rest content,
It is its own advertisement.

'The perpetual scapegoat, trussed up once and for all in the Nuremberg Laws . . . is . . . dragged out and punished over and over again.' — *New York Times*, June 22nd.

Caesars in Rome's Imperial seat
Fed lions Early Christian meat,
But folk of the New Testament
Rome counted less than one per cent.
And thus, despite official care
Not every lion got his share.

So now the nobler Nazi lion
Who mauls the naked flesh of Zion,
And for his German birthright claims
State quarry for the Streicher Games,
Though roaring for the tribal sport,
Like Caesar's King of Beasts, goes short.

The Reich preserves her Jews to kick
All round the body politic,
But folk of the Old Testament
Are counted less than one per cent,
So after each prescribed abuse
They are thrashed home for future use.

The Reich can therefore not discuss
Facilities for Exodus,
For if no Jew were left behind,
But just the Nazi and his kind,
What pastime could he practise then
To show himself the King of Men?

# FRITTO MISTO

'The Italian race has remained pure for the last 2000 years.' — *La Difesa della Razza*, Rome.

When Alaric mopped up in Rome
With his totalitarians,
Italian dames were not at home
To visiting barbarians,
Disdaining to supply the Goth
With Teuton offspring hardy,
As later they withheld their troth
From lovesick Langobardi.

Their way was equally abrupt
With overlords Byzantine,
Lest Roman blood they might corrupt
With influence levantine.
These steadfast virgins spurned like dirt
The decadent Hellenic,
And never would so much as flirt
With Emirs Saracenic.

Invaders of two thousand years,
Not always of the purest,
Left fewer racial souvenirs
Than any summer tourist.
The mothers of the Coming Race
Abhorred miscegenation
And substituted in its place
Parthenogeneration.

Thus their posterity retains
No trace of alien foemen,
Not Fifty-Seven Heinz-like strains
But just the antique Roman!
So Fascists learn eugenic lore
And racial boloney
And hope to look like Caesar more,
And less like Al Capone.

## ADVICE TO AGGRESSORS

Meine Herren and Signori,
Clients of the British Tory,
Kindly note that Number 10
Asks your patronage again.
Opening, as from to-day,
As Chamberlain et Daladier,
Messrs. Hoare, Laval, successors,
For doing business with aggressors.

Frontiers promptly liquidated,
Coups d'état consolidated,
Pledges taken and exchanged,
Acquisitions rearranged,
Loans on Fascist risks advanced,
Nazi enterprise financed,
European intervention
Given personal attention.
Have you problems of Partition?
Let us send a British Mission.

Breaking with Geneva's firms,
We offer Nazis favoured terms;
Let us lend to back your claim
England's honourable name,
For dirty deals both great and small
Our representative will call.
Orders carried out with speed,
Satisfaction guaranteed.
We obsequiously remain,
Daladier et Chamberlain.


## WILL YOU, WON'T YOU?

'There is reason to suspect that both Great Britain and France were preparing to bring yet more pressure on the Czechs. This is behind the French suggestion that Lord Runciman should be asked to produce yet another plan.' — Vernon Bartlett, (*News Chronicle*, Sept. 15th).

'Will you give a little farther?' said his lordship to the Czechs,
'There's a gentleman behind us I should really hate to vex,
I have taken on a mission to maintain the open door,
So to prove co-operation will you give a little more?
Will you, won't you, will you, won't you give a little more?

'I shall use to your advantage every token of goodwill,
So do your part by giving way a little farther still.'
Then said the Czechs, 'Our formulas already number four.'
And they thanked his lordship kindly but could not give any more,
Could not, would not, could not, would not give a little more.

His lordship said, 'You've no idea how lovely it would be,
If you'd just give way completely and leave all the rest to me;
The fruitful paths of compromise I would again explore,
(As a purely private person), if you gave a little more.
Will you, won't you, will you, won't you give a little more?'

The Czechs said mediation would be greatly simplified,
If concessions were requested in a quarter still untried,
His lordship answered that this view he must indeed deplore,
If they found themselves unable to concede a little more,
If they would not, could not, would not, could not give a little
more.

He pointed out how steadily and surely they'd advance,
Secure in the assurances of Britain and of France,
But they answered in a strain that shocked his lordship to the
core,
That they feared non-intervention if they gave a little more,
So would not, could not, would not, could not give a little
more.

# THE DESCENT OF MAN

'An emergency trench . . . can be rapidly made in a garden. The depth suggested is 4ft. 6in. The roof should slope slightly so that rain-water may drain off and should be covered with two or three inches of earth to hold it down.' — *The Times*, Sept. 26th.

> For this, man's handiwork was wrought,
> For this he heavenward aspired,
> For this his philosophic thought
> Of universal truth inquired,
> And all his science comes to this
> Derogatory Nemesis.
>
> The long achievement of the mind,
> The Law's majestic edifice,
> Arts for man's benefit designed,
> All time's inventions come to this,
> That people with immortal souls
> Must crawl like beetles into holes.
>
> Emancipated from the ape
> So long to wear creation's crown,
> A little surface soil we scrape
> And living in the earth lie down,
> Abandoning the godlike view
> To squirm below as vermin do.
>
> With drains and ditches for our tomb
> We scurry underground to hide,
> And there await the insect's doom,
> In torrents of insecticide,
> As man's exterminating bomb
> Rounds off his epic martyrdom.

'After all, there are no secrets now about what happened in the air and in the mobilization of our anti-aircraft defences . . . Who pretends that our anti-aircraft defences were adequately manned or armed? . . . There has been a gross neglect and deficiency in our defences.' — Mr. Churchill, House of Commons, Oct. 5th.

Give thanks to all who sidetracked war,
To each peacemaking hero,
When every hope appeared to mock,
When pacifism died of shock,
When even the deaf could hear the clock
Already striking zero.

So to Daladier, give thanks,
Give Chamberlain his statue,
To Mussolini, aiding both,
Vote heartfelt thanks, however loath,
For bounding from the undergrowth
To circumvent the *battue*.

For his great part give Benes thanks,
Give Roosevelt acclamation
That Mars is cheated of his feast,
That we ourselves are not deceased,
That Prague has not been made at least
The pyre of Czech cremation.

Thank all who steered our peaceward course
And all who keep it steady,
Thank our own backbone, Britain's boast,
And thank our Navy at its post,
But thank Sir Thomas Inskip most
Because he was not ready

# UNDER WHICH FLAG?

## [*After Rudyard Kipling*]

'Uncertainty as to the future sovereignty of Tanganyika Territory is destroying its social and economic structure . . . The Government are fully aware of the uncertainty and anxiety . . . but they are not in a position to add to the pronouncements which have been made in the past.' — *The Times*, Oct. 25th.

'A resolution was passed that a declaration should be sent to the King, if the Imperial Government did not within a short space of time announce that Tanganyika, now held under a League Mandate, would become a British Colony.' — *Daily Telegraph*, Nov. 1st.

Lords of Whitehall, give answer! They are whinnying to and fro,
And how can they answer at Whitehall what only the Führer can
    know?
Shall a rabble of rascal planters create a colonial snag?
They are lifting their heads in the stillness to yelp for the English flag!

Never a shore so thriving, where the Reich flag once was flown
But, forfeit of Britain's Empire, the Third Reich claims for its own,
Unfurling its standards to follow a Goebbelized plebescite
From the waters of Lake Tanganyika to Kilimanjaro's height.

While big breeds arm and chaffer, while lesser breeds are swapped,
Shall mandatees of the run-down League discover their right to opt?
The swastika swings to the zenith; the Führer screams to the mike;
And Whitehall stands to the halliards, waiting the word to strike.

Is the jackal robbed of its meat, is the weasel baulked of its prey?
They ha' cursed the loss of the Southern Cross and who shall say them
    nay?
They may not ask of England; they are whinnying to and fro!
But how can Whitehall answer, when Whitehall does not know?

## THE REASON

A rather extreme vegetarian,
Looked down from his summit Bavarian,
    He said: 'It's not odd
    I'm superior to God,
For the Latter's not even an Aryan.'


## ALTERNATIVES

For the Duce's inflated ideas
We can offer but two panaceas —
Either give him Gibraltar,
Suez, Cyprus, and Malta,
Or a kick in the Pantellarias.


## DE MORTUIS NIL NISI MALUM

'The League . . . identified change with aggression, forgetting that
what is called aggression may be the only remedy against . . . injustice.' — Scrutator, *Sunday Times*, Jan. 15th.

With every diminishing Session
The League is more clearly to blame
For classing as acts of aggression
The Fascist's legitimate claim;
The habit of joint accusations
At each insignificant rape
Provoking the mass violations
Now changing the Continent's shape.

This ideologic position
Could not but alarm and estrange
Ex-members who urged recognition
For armed methods of peaceable change.
Now causes of crisis are fewer
While peace remains almost intact,
Much water has flowed through the sewer
Since Laval sold the League for a pact.

The League was a palpable blunder,
A perfectly hopeless ideal,
The Covenant doomed to go under
Once realists dared to be real.
Geneva is dead, damned and rotten,
Appeasement will yet save our skin —
So perhaps it is better forgotten
That the League put the Government in.


## ONCE MORE UNTO THE PEACE

'Mr. Chamberlain always travels with a pocket Shakespeare.' —
*Daily Telegraph*, Feb. 23rd.

Once more unto the peace, dear friends, once more,
And wean aggressors with our English gold!
Costly our armament as purse can buy,
For, while we are in silken dalliance led,
Come the Dictators of the world in arms,
And they will shock us; they will shock this England,
This precious stone set in a sea of troubles.
Let me with cyphers for this great accompt
On your imaginary terrors work,
While armourers are closing up the gaps
With note of aimless preparation.

You all know this umbrella: I remember
When first I flew with it to Berchtesgaden,
The day I overthrew democracy,
For thine especial safety. Follow it!
It beckons you, a most miraculous organ,
And none so Left but does it reverence.
See these few precepts we in memory keep.
Give every man our voice but few our aid:
Be ever strong upon the stronger side:
This above all — to our own class be true;
And it must follow, as the boom the slump,
We cannot then astonish any man.
Methinks I am a prophet new-inspired!
Friends, Britons, countrymen, lend me your cash;
Cry 'Jitterbug!' and pay the price of peace
To profiteers, gaping for increment.


## NO OBLIGATION

'It will be generally agreed that there is no . . . obligation upon the
British Government to take any direct action in the present develop-
ments in Central Europe.' — *The Times*, March 14th.

Czechoslovakia meets her fate
Disarmed, enslaved and carved in three.
Though Britain guaranteed the State
No State exacts a guarantee
When it has ceased to be.

Through Munich, Prague, and yet beyond
Appeasement's path must be pursued;
Democracy need not despond
While Briton's word is still as good
As Hitler's bond.

Though tolerant in deed and word
Of Powers that murder, cheat and lie,
Our hands are clean, our purpose high,
And through the world our voice is heard —
Live and let die!


## STANDING FIRM

'The annexation of Czechoslovakia may be the act of a much-worried man in a hurry.' — Scrutator in *Sunday Times*, March 26th.

When Führers lie, it's something of a shock
And budding shoots of confidence are bruised,
While rumours of a democratic *bloc*
Attest to counsels wild and minds confused;
But after some few days of taking stock
The inexcusable may be excused,
(Though certain Powers would advocate suppression
Suppose another ventured on aggression).

Encirclement is not Great Britain's end,
Nor is collective action her design,
But to inquire on whom she might depend
In case the situation should decline,
And she herself be called on to defend
Herself, if menaced from beyond the Rhine,
(Though by no means at one with world opinion
That any single Power seeks world dominion).

Great Britain takes her stand on right and law,
Condoning breaches with unfeigned regret,
And neither will the outstretched hand withdraw,
And neither truckle to the naked threat.

Some final provocation, or last straw
She waits, which has not been presented yet,
Resolved meantime to go to any distance
To fortify the line of least resistance.


## SEEDS OF LOVE
*[Acknowledgments to Macdonald and Tate]*

'The British Ambassador, Sir William Seeds, had another talk with
the Foreign Commissar, M. Litvinoff.' — Moscow wire, *Daily Telegraph*, April 22nd.

### VERSE
Loving hearts are sundered in London and Berlin,
Discords mar love's sweet refrain;
Chamberlain is striving coy Stalin's heart to win
As he tells the old, old story once again.
Though he feel dismay at true love's delay
And the steppes are freezing hard,
His tender questionnaire
Is heard upon the air
In tones of almost diffident regard:

### CHORUS
'If I should plant my tiny Seeds of love
In the garden of your heart,
Would they grow to be a great big pact one day
And frighten the Axis right away,
Would you trust in me as far as you could see,
(Ideologies apart,)
If I should plant my tiny Seeds of love
In the garden of your heart?'

252

# THE DIEHARD'S FAREWELL

Turn my face to St. James's as falls the eventide
They will hear at the Club to-morrow how a Tory Diehard died;
Give me my port and coffee and my favourite cigar
And round my knees wrap the panther rug I potted in Coosh Behar.
Here's my letter to tell *The Times* how a Diehard took to bed
The day he heard a Tory chief would make a pact with the Red.

Pass the Napoleon brandy, my strength is failing fast,
The country bound for the dogs so long has gone to the dogs at last,
Not by a Liberal hothead, not by a Labour cad,
But by a Conservative Premier stabbed in the back, by Gad!
I've kept a stiff upper lip through life, a Diehard born and bred,
But even a Diehard dies at last when they make a pact with the Red.

# THE TRUSTEE

'The well-being and development of people not yet able to stand
by themselves is a sacred trust of civilization.' — Lord Halifax, June 30th.
'I don't feel happy about the way our power is being used in the
West Indies and other parts.' — Ramsay Muir, Aug. 9th.

    Wherever flies the Union Jack
    In warm Imperial air,
    All races yellow, brown and black
    The Briton's birthright share.
    And he who fights for subjects' rights
    Is not accused of wrong,
Excepting perhaps in Mauritius, Jamaica, the Gold Coast, Sierra Leone,
    Rhodesia, North Borneo, Antigua and Hong-kong.

Where the Colonial Office rules
O'er palmy tropic scenes,
No subject learns at Mission schools
What exploitation means.
No laws prevent their betterment,
Free speech is smiled upon,
Excepting perhaps in Burma, Cyprus, Nigeria, Trinidad, Malaya,
Sarawak, St. Helena and Ceylon.

Where Britain for the Empire's good
Performs her sacred trust,
Crude problems of wage servitude
Need never be discussed.
Rule that reveals her high ideals
The whole world venerates,
With the possible exception of the Continent of Europe, the Soviet,
the Near East, the Far East, South America, Mexico and the United
States.


NERVES

[Sept. 2nd, 1939]

I think I'll get a paper,
I think I'd better wait.
I'll hear the news at six o'clock,
That's much more up to date.

It's just like last September,
Absurd how time stands still;
They're bound to make a statement.
I don't suppose they will.

I think I'd better stroll around.
Perhaps it's best to stay.
I think I'll have a whisky neat,
I can't this time of day.

I think I'll have another smoke.
I don't know what to do.
I promised to ring someone up,
I can't remember who.

They say it's been averted.
They say we're on the brink.
I'll wait for the 'New Statesman',
I wonder what they think.

They're shouting. It's a Special.
It's not. It's just street cries.
I think the heat is frightful.
God damn these bloody flies.

I see the nation's keeping cool,
The public calm is fine.
This crisis can't shake England's nerves.
It's playing hell with mine.

# COMMAND PERFORMANCE

At 9 a.m., September 1st, 1939, German bombers attack Polish towns.

'Let there be war' he said and as he spoke
The war cloud broke.
Alone he launched upon the swelling scene
The war machine,
And so upon the last of Hitler's shows
The curtain rose.

The act unfolds. Reich bandsmen plug once more
The hackneyed score,
The strutting Führer postures in the lead,
Spotlit Siegfried,
While to accompany his world-famed turn,
Ships drown, homes burn.

Reich supers hail the conflagration vast
As unsurpassed,
But we who watch with less admiring eyes
The curtain rise
Make known the Führer will not take the call
When it shall fall.

# HOME SERVICE

8 a.m.

'There is no new French communiqué.
In well-informed circles they say
Trade talks may soon be under way,
But we cannot yet ascertain whose.
The Council of War has conferred.
Some gunfire by neutrals was heard.
Some action at outposts occurred.
And that's the end of the news.

1 p.m.

'An Agency message last night
Describes a reconnaissance flight,
But over what ground, at what height,
There are so far (I'm sorry) no clues.
Off Sweden some smoke has been seen
Which may indicate some submarine.
On the Western Front all is serene.
And that's the end of the news.

4 p.m.

'Information has just been supplied
Camouflage has been recently tried
Our Air Force positions to hide,
(A highly ingenious ruse).
From France strict reserve is maintained,
Some gunfire has not been explained.
It has semi-officially rained.
And that's the end of the news.

6 p.m.

'In the communiqué we repeat
Official reserve is complete.
According to Reuter, the Fleet
Has captured (I'm sorry) some crews.
Reconnaissance flights have been flown,
Important results have been shown.
The Market closed firmer in tone.
And that's the end of the news.

9 p.m.

'Some talks are proceeding somewhere.
We are ready by land, sea and air.
The War Council has met to compare
Completely identical views.
The French communiqué on the war
States that all is the same as before.
(I'm sorry, I'll read that once more)
And that's the end of the news.'


## WAR ECONOMY

Now England has pooled her resources
And the national effort directs,
While her children join up with the forces
With the *élan* that England expects,
Not all can be marching and drilling
But all can show *esprit de corps*,
We others are cheerful and willing
But we cannot get into the war.

We can help by not showing resistance
To authoritarian control,
Till all are on public assistance
Excepting for those on the dole;
We can help in the nation's endeavour
By enrolling as never before,
But the lists are all full up for ever,
So we cannot get into the war.

We can help by an effort concerted
In directions officially shown
Till everyone's debts are converted
For investment in Government Loan,
For the finding of millions and millions,
And billions and trillions more
Is the only job left for civilians
Who cannot get into the war.

No tittle our firmness relaxes
Till justice (with peace) we restore,
But we can't raise the cash for the taxes
If we cannot get into the war.


A SCIENTIFIC ARM

'What, teacher, can that object be inside a plate-glass drum?'
'It is Professor Haldane whom you see, testing a vacuum.'

'Why are they hurling bombs so near that shelter made of tin?'
'That is a bombproof test, I hear, Professor Haldane is within.'

'Oh, look! From yon balloon so high what dangles large and limp?'
'It is Professor Haldane, we espy, air testing from a blimp.'

'See drifting near the waterside that buoy of strange design!'
'That is Professor Haldane, tied, decoying of a mine.

'On sea, on shore and in the air, protecting us from harm,
Professor Haldane meets us everywhere — our scientific arm.'


## PEACE AIM

'I am inclined to think the Führer knows his Germans. Amongst the masses who have nothing at stake there is observable a certain amount of *Schadenfreude*.'
'Recent events have revealed to me a facet of the German character which I had not suspected ... This outbreak of sadistic cruelty.' — Extracts from White Paper, Germany No. 2, 1939.

When the war has been finally won,
We are counselled in speeches and sermons,
To make certain that nothing is done
To wound or discourage the Germans.
We must strictly exclude from our aims
Suspicion of punitive measures,
But how can we deal with their claims
To their popular national pleasures?

When regenerate Germany asks,
On resumption of friendly relations,
To shoulder her share of the tasks
That are common to civilized nations,
Can her people abandon the cult
In which they so gleefully revelled
With the not unpredicted result
That they're morally somewhat dishevelled?

What pastimes and games will be left
If humans no longer are hounded,
And arson and slander and theft
By legal deterrents surrounded?
Must they close down their torture-resorts
So greatly enjoyed by S.A. boys
And spoil the legitimate sports
Of Himmler's uproarious playboys?

When the Nazis are held a disgrace
And a scapegoat is made of their saviour,
Can we hope that this thoroughbred race
Will abandon Germanic behaviour?
When even his critics concede
That what made his régime so successful
Was his sense of his countrymen's need
For a hearty debauch in the cesspool?

While we own admiration extreme
For the Germans' historical glories,
Their manner of letting off steam
Shows something's gone wrong with their *mores*;
Their title may not be denied
To their *lieder*, their lager, their treasures,
But can civilization provide
For their rather peculiar pleasures?

'It resolves itself into a question of supply and demand. The unforeseen lull in the opening stages of the war has not created the anticipated demand. We have not had long lists of casualties leaving serious gaps in the commissioned ranks ... hence discontent amongst officer reserves at home.' – War Office Departmental Chief (*Daily Telegraph*, Feb. 12th).

When the gallant ex-officer craves a commission
And meets with a frigid official response,
It means that the war of blockade and attrition
Has no need of his gallantry just for the nonce.
The lag has a perfectly logical reason,
It is merely a case of demand and supplies,
The cannon refusing their fodder this season
The looked-for emergency does not arise.

The War on the West Front is one of those gambles,
With no one proposing the slightest advance,
But until the whole line is a bit of a shambles
There's not even standing-room 'somewhere in France'.
Every foot of the front is successfully guarded,
Inaction proceeds in a regular groove,
But the call to reservists is *pro tem.* retarded
Till someone shows symptoms of making a move.

So ex-heroes, debarred from the theatre of action,
Mope far from the scenes where the battle should be,
Where visiting War Lords express satisfaction
And bugles are blowing for ENSA and tea.
Their rush to the Colours is brusquely arrested
By the widespread display of the War Office sign –
*Allied field of glory completely congested,*
*No vacancies left in the Maginot Line.*

# THE SUITS OF WOE

'The people of this country are united with sympathy for the
situation in which they find themselves, and in admiration for the
courage with which they have maintained for so long in the struggle
against overwhelming odds. This epic story ... will remain alive
in the memory of all people.' — Prime Minister on Finland, March 13th.

The hour brings forth the man. This iron time
Which tolls the knell of nation after nation,
Demands, as victims of each murderous crime
Are shuffled off to hasty inhumation,
A master of the simple yet sublime
To standardize the funeral oration,
And in this species of non-stop recital
The world yields Chamberlain unchallenged title.

As to their rest the gashed remains are borne,
Securely nailed inside the flag-draped coffin,
His graveside tributes to all those that mourn
The sharpness of bereavement needs must soften.
The weeds of woe were never better worn —
The trouble is, he wears them much too often
And sometimes spreads consolatory unction
At a not strictly necessary function.

When one in so commanding a position
Shows such obituary eloquence,
There comes a moment in the repetition
When there must burst upon the dullest sense
A wild but uncontrollable suspicion
It may not all be pure coincidence,
But Fate mows down these nations small and gallant
To exercise an elegiac talent.

From which there follows, none knows why or how,
Upon these obsequies, the firm conviction
That we should not perpetually endow
This hoary mourner, this confirmed affliction
Whose term of office has been up to now,
Despite his own unjustified prediction
And notwithstanding pacts of mutual amity,
A chronicle of unrelieved calamity.

No man is ever England's Premier named
Without some attribute of highest order,
Then how shall Mr. Chamberlain be famed
By history, time's impartial recorder,
Who for so long memorially framed
His era in a double mourning border?
As stern War Minister? or blest peacemaker?
Or just a universal undertaker?

## REVENONS A NOS MOUTONS

'Civilians complain . . . there is too much mutton and too little beef
. . . nearly all is commandeered for the troops. Representations are
being made to the War Office to take a greater proportion of mutton.'
— *Daily Telegraph*, April 1st.

Breathes there the man with soul so dead
Who would not be on mutton fed
To save his own, his native land!
Whose palate shrinks, whose stomach turns,
Who his official ration spurns,
Who asks for beef when beef is banned!

If such there are (and such there be)
Their taste amounts to treachery,
Raw joints thrown back upon the State
Unseasonable glut create.
We grow like that which we devour
And in this world-decisive hour
The roast beef of Old England's might
Befits the soldier's appetite,
Civilians must to mutton keep
Becoming more and more like sheep.

\* \* \*

Commend O Reith, this prudent course
The home front from its torpor shake,
The vigour of our rump-fed force
Is worth an age without a steak!


# O GOD! O WASHINGTON!

## [*After Samuel Butler*]

'The German record ... makes neutrality not merely difficult for
Americans but shameful as well.' — Westbrook Pegler, U.S. columnist.

Far away in the United States of America
The Isolationists bury their heads in the sand, saying:
'The belligerents are six of one and half-a-dozen of the other,
But great is the Monroe Doctrine, rich the blessings of abstract
    neutrality,'
    O God! O Washington!

Neutral through thick and thin in the old brave battle for freedom
They voted credits to Finland solely for agricultural implements
While trading arms to all comers on a cash-and-carry basis
That they might be without reproach in the sight of the aggressors.
    O God! O Washington!

265

And the voice of reason crieth to the Isolationists, saying:
Ye who prefer the gabble of Goebbels to the gospel of freedom,
When Britain is Hitler's doormat and France Mussolini's cuspidor,
Think ye to escape a kick on your large white naked posteriors?
            O God! O Washington!

But the voice of reason falleth unheard on the Isolationists' posteriors
The elevation of which blasphemes the principles of democracy.
Geese once saved Rome but the ostriches of the Capitol will not save
    America.
O Thomas Jefferson! O Walt Whitman! O Henry James! O President
    Roosevelt!
            O Washington! O God!


## THE LEADER

They prayed for one to guide and lead,
He came at last unheralded
To give his people in their need
Work, peace and bread.

He warmed them at the fires of hate,
He fed them on imagined wrong,
He made the race inviolate,
Feared, safe and strong.

Evil with good he reconciled,
They for his blessings sacrificed
Daughters and sons, the unborn child,
The creed of Christ.

He showed earth's kingdoms spread below,
He scaled the height; they headlong fell
The soul's and body's death to know
And war's unutterable hell.

266

# WHO WILL BE SATISFIED?

If Germany cast out the fiend
And stood upon the angel's side,
From lust of domination weaned,
But still secured in strength and pride,
The English would be satisfied.

If she retired beyond the Rhine,
Which must the Reich from France divide,
(Content her conquests to resign)
And in her bounds in peace to bide,
The French would then be satisfied.

If when the terms of peace are made
America might serve as guide,
Ensuring transatlantic trade
(Free competition not denied),
The States would be quite satisfied.

But if the race we fight to save
Should over victory preside,
If Poland, rising from the grave
Should sit between the Powers allied,
How shall the Poles be satisfied?

For stricken towns and pillaged lands,
For plague and famine far and wide,
For slavery at German hands,
For the red death that Poland died,
How shall the Poles be satisfied?

Till hate itself shall cease to be,
Till German crimes by Poles are tried,
Till there is no more Germany,
Till Poland's blood and tears are dried,
How shall the Poles be satisfied?

# ANTICLIMAX ON THE RUBICON

As far as to the Rubicon
Caesar advances in his stride,
His dauntless legions egg him on,
Fate beckons from the farther side;
Armed at all points for total war
He bivouacs upon the shore.

Long has he stropped the eagles' beaks,
Long blown victorious bugle calls,
His cohorts now for weeks and weeks
Have pasted posters up on walls.
The hour decisive and sublime
Is here — and has been for some time.

Caesar surveys the scheduled leap,
Resolved to gamble — on a cert;
Born for the toga's ampler sweep
Yet loath to lose the Fascist shirt.
Great Caesar of the Fascist brand,
We understand, we understand.

We know why destiny delays
Until Rome's triumph is prepared,
We wait the last dynamic phase,
We see Rome's stainless cleaver bared.
Go, brag before your roaring boys,
The world is weary of your noise.

Rome's pickings may be kept or lost,
Her world-decisive hour has passed,
The Rubicon by others crossed
The fatal die by others cast,
Your lightnings miss, your thunder's jammed —
Cross, Mussolini, and be damned!

# INAUGURAL ELEGY

'By arming the people you run risks. Innocent people may be accidentally killed. That doesn't matter if the nation is saved.' — T. L. Horabin, M.P., *News Chronicle*, June 18th.

The curfew does not knell the parting day,
The lowing herd skedaddle from the lea,
The plowman leaps the stile to get away,
And leaves the village to the L.D.V.[1]

The glimmering landscape hums with hand grenades,
The squire instructs his squad with simple skill,
The busy housewife builds the barricades,
The rude grandfathers of the hamlet drill.

By yonder lych-gate's ivy-mantled arch
The vicar kindles tar and paraffin,
Which, meant to halt the invader's armoured march,
May make one half the county 'next of kin'.

The blunderbus speaks from the twitt'ring clump
And wings the beetle on his wonted flight,
Age gets entangled in the stirrup-pump
And infancy hurls sticks of dynamite.

Far from anticipated zones of strife,
The village that upon itself relies
(With some inevitable loss of life)
Is not, like armies, taken by surprise.

And if some wanderer, innocent of blame,
Receive the passing tribute of a shot
With stern resolve discharged but random aim,
This uncouth rhyme one day will mark the spot.

[1] Local Defence Volunteers, afterwards renamed Home Guard.

Somewhere beneath this animated scene
There lies a swain who straggled from the road.
Shun, reader, like the plague, the village green
And shelter, trembling, in thine own abode.


## ALL QUIET
### [*June 23rd*, 1940]

We can take down the map of the war
With the sweep of the Maginot Line
Broad and strong from the sea to the Rhine,
And the cities, the rivers, the forts.
There is no Western Front any more,
The Line was a sham after all.
We shall hear no more 'latest reports'
We can take down the map from the wall.

These cities have gone up in flames,
These cornlands and vineyards are lost,
The Marne and the Seine have been crossed,
There is nothing left now but the names,
The rivers are full of the dead.
It was here the tanks broke through the Gap,
Here they stood, here they fell, here they fled.
It is done. We can take down the map.

The battle is suddenly still,
The life is gone out of the land,
Consigned to the enemy's hand,
Betrayed and surrendered and sold
To be tamed to the conqueror's will.

Now silence and terror descend,
Our friend and our comrade of old
Will not be at our side to the end.

We can take down the map of the war,
From the Rhône and the Rhine to the sea
All's quiet as the grave; there will be
No counter-attack or advance.
The flag is defiled that she bore
And the sword of her forging is blunt.
So peace has been given to France,
All's quiet on the Western Front.


## MINISTRY MYSTERY

'49 persons in the Ministry of Information receive salaries of £1,000
a year, and over.' —*Hansard*, Aug. 7th.

Though national safety must comment disarm
It may never be perfectly clear
Why some get a fortnight for spreading alarm
While some get a thousand a year.

# NOTHING ALIEN IS HUMAN

'Soon, very soon, the sun will rise again and shine ... we shall call at the chosen moment to all whom Hitler enslaved and tortured to rise.' — Dr. Hugh Dalton, Broadcast, Aug. 11th.

When Ministers prophetically call
To friendly aliens conquered and oppressed,
Their orotund asseverations fall
A trifle flat, it has to be confessed,
While they, proclaiming liberty for all,
The champions of liberty arrest;
And even to the friendliest alien ear
Their words sound relatively insincere.

The friendly alien fails to understand
Why, when enslaved, we name them our allies,
Their kindred in our own crusading land
We class as suspects, saboteurs and spies;
So when at our benevolent command
The sun of freedom once again shall rise
They may not credit the phenomenon
But ask whose side it will be shining on.

When we intern the friends of liberty
We cancel Ministerial eloquence,
When we deport the alien refugee
We shake the friendly alien's confidence,
Until between us and the enemy
They find in fact so little difference
That when we sound the hour of their release
They may be reconciled to Nazi peace.

Though with the tongue of angels and of men
Our cause to liberty we dedicate,
Till England to herself is true again
And those unjustly held we liberate,
So long as to the friendly alien
Fear and mistrust our policy dictate,
It seems, at least to aliens, a mistake
To say that Britain fights for freedom's sake.


## I WILL ARISE

### [After W. B. Yeats]

I will arise and go now, and seek a Ministry,
And a deep shelter find there of ferro-concrete made,
The Departmental personnel will all make room for me,
And I shall sleep through the b—— loud raid.

Yes, I shall wait for peace there, for peace keeps stopping short,
Stopping for the wail of warning that noon and darkness brings;
Here midnight's all a-jitter with the A.A. guns' report
And evening full of the Luftwaffe's wings.

I will arise and go now, for wandering astray
I hear from Whitehall's refuges that long untroubled snore;
As I duck in surface shelters the Blitz can blast away,
I hear it in the deep earth's core.

# WHO SHALL WASH THE RHINE?

*'Ye Nymphs that reign o'er sewers and sinks,*
*The river Rhine, it is well known,*
*Doth wash your city of Cologne;*
*But tell me, Nymphs! what power divine*
*Shall henceforth wash the river Rhine?'*

Samuel Taylor Coleridge

## ST GEORGE AND THE DRAGON

St George has taken up the sword,
And keeps unsleeping watch and ward,
To liberate from vile duress
The Dragon's victims in distress.
Surrounded by his knights and squires
He kindles Britain's martial fires,
While all the busy island stirs,
Loud with the hum of armourers,
Loud with the hammer on the forge
Shaping the harness of St George,
And even louder with the sound
Of private axes being ground.
Three years his brandished blade has waved,
To lead a Continent enslaved
(Though he has not essayed a sortie
Since France sold out, in nineteen-forty).
While royal heralds from Whitehall
Blow an incessant bugle call,
While old War Office chargers neigh,
Snuffing afar the armoured fray,
While artisans in workshops toil,
And hinds plough up the scanty soil,
Preserved in their beleaguered fort,
As in the days of Agincourt,

From rapine, slavery and slaughter,
By several lucky leagues of water.
But still the Dragon mauls his prize,
And Britain's chivalry defies,
Till certain Paladins confess
Doubts of the champion's success
Against a foe in nowise bound
By customs of the Table Round,
Who, being duly cleft in twain,
Returns to baleful life again,
With more efficient claws and scales
And twice as many heads and tails;
Who, after every *coup-de-grâce*,
Leads knighthood to a fresh *impasse*
From which they may no exit seek
By the Arthurian technique.
The leader of the sceptic knights,
Far-famed as the Vansittartites,
Admonishes the Saint at war,
He scotched the Dragon once before,
But lacked the necessary will
The monster once for all to kill.
'This cockatrice that now we face,
Is totem of a savage race,
Known since the time of Tacitus
As bloody, starved and ravenous,
Who blasted with Teutonic rage
The sunset of the Roman Age,
Who with their sanguinary mark
Made the so-called Dark Ages dark,
Who revelled in aggressive wars
Of Holy Roman Emperors,
Whose savagery was renewed
Through centuries of tribal feud,
Dynastic and domestic broil

Congenial to their blood and soil,
Until two thousand years of hate,
Dammed up within the Prussian State,
By ruthless war-lords trained and led,
With greed inflamed, with envy fed,
At last, like Wotan's bolt was hurled
To burn and devastate the world.
This human spawn of dragon seed
Perpetuates the dragon breed.
The Teuton monster now abroad
Is famed no less for force than fraud,
A very prodigy of guile,
It weeps like any crocodile,
And oft has tempted to its den
Good, simple, Christian gentlemen,
Who most unfortunately went
And sealed their own predicament.
St George this hydra cannot fight
With weapons of a Red Cross knight,
The Dragon with the Folk is one,
No separate phenomenon,
And knighthood on its sacred oath
Must settle finally with both.'
So speaks Sir Robert, and his word
Is far beyond the ramparts heard,
Albeit St George makes no reply,
His stainless broadsword whirling high,
Being dedicated to his mission
But tongue-tied by a Coalition.
Eftsoon there charge into the lists
Vansittart's shocked antagonists,
Who claim the Champion's other ear,
And call on all good men to hear.
'Sir Robert's views' they cry 'in sooth,
Are minus all objective truth,

His history is crass distortion,
His mind devoid of true proportion,
His premisses mere fallacies,
His helmet is a hive for bees,
His mischievous hypothesis
Leads to the ultimate abyss.
The Teuton nation, like our own,
Has long its backward past outgrown,
And boasts an honourable part
In realms of science and of art.
The name, barbarian, must appal
A folk so truly musical,
Whose daily life is interwoven
With Bach, with Mozart and Beethoven,
And whose distinguished literature
Their claim to culture must assure.
We fight, but with a long-term aim,
This seeming Dragon to reclaim,
Remembering its origins
In British, not in German, sins,
For it was generated by
The gross injustice of Versailles,
Its dread appearance a reminder
We should be, not more harsh, but kinder.
Its mangled prey we must release,
But after, with itself make peace,
Abandoning the use of force
In floods of mutual remorse.
If one hand wield the righteous blade,
The other must apply first aid,
And offer a deranged society
The ministrations of psychiatry.
This monster is, the truth to tell,
A dachshund under wizard spell,
Which will its proper shape resume

When the magician meets his doom.
The Germans, a deluded nation,
Knew nothing of the transformation,
For when the Dragon started roaring
They were all fast asleep and snoring.
This hell-hound's crimes are none of theirs,
It burst upon them unawares.
Then do not chivalry disgrace
By condemnation of a race,
Nor in uncharitable mood
With Germans bad damn Germans good,
But let St George forthwith proclaim
Monster and men are not the same,
And make it known beyond the seas
We recognize two Germanies!'
Thus while far off great battles rage,
These knights in private tilts engage,
Fling down the glove, and lances break
In argument for its own sake,
By their diversionary action
Revealing Britain's soul of faction;
For Britons in the jaws of death
On controversy spend their breath,
And even as they fight for life
Can never cease from mental strife.
Barred from political abuse
By reason of a Party truce,
The ruling passion finds its vent
In dialectic argument,
The champions giving blow for blow,
For and against their mortal foe.
'Avenge! avenge!' the realists cry,
'Lest you should see your children die!'
The idealists retort 'Forgive!
If you would see your children live.'

One side declares that it rejoices
To hear in the Third Reich two voices,
The other hears in tones yet clearer,
One voice: 'One Reich, one folk, one Führer!'
Both factions summon their supporters
From likely and unlikely quarters
And call to this abstruse debate
The mediocre and the great,
The sage, the savant, the professor,
Great intellectual lights and lesser,
Loquacious ex-ambassadors,
Discursive neutral travellers,
Reich somebodies, Reich nobodies,
Right émigrés, Left refugees,
Whose diatribes against delusion
Complete the general confusion,
As mutual errors they discuss
With unrelenting animus.
Both sides depict for Britons' study
The German mild, the German bloody,
The German past, the German present,
The German pleasant and unpleasant,
The boastful German, and the doleful,
The soulless German, and the soulful,
The German wolves, the German asses,
The German chiefs, the German masses,
The German baffling comprehension,
Are forced on popular attention
As if this everlasting topic
All matters else made microscopic,
As if the German soul to learn
Were Britain's paramount concern,
As if the course of future history
Depended on some German mystery
And hung on Englishmen agreeing

About the Teuton's inmost being,
From century to century
A strictly unknown quantity,
Which to the riddle holds the clue —
Is there one Reich? or are there two?
And yet, to those who care to look,
The German is an open book,
For never did the Teuton tribes
Have any lack of bards, or scribes,
But ever have themselves depicted
With copiousness unrestricted,
Since no vicissitude can cure
Their *penchant* for self-portraiture.
No people so extremely voluble
Presents a mystery insoluble,
And Germans though they bore and weary us
Are not, in fact, at all mysterious.
The German's a recurrent danger,
But he is in himself no stranger.
Alone of European lands
His country Britain understands,
His blood has kinship with our own,
His kings have sat upon our throne,
His soldiers have our battles fought,
His thought has influenced our thought,
And certain Britons counted wise
Have seen the world through German eyes.
All types of Germans high and low,
Of old the British people know;
The high-born *noblesse* of the past,
The high-born military caste,
The high-born Junker autocrat,
The lumpish proletariat,
The still more lumpish bourgeoisie,
The ultra-lumpish peasantry,

The low-born and industrious swarm
Who dearly love a uniform,
All born and bred to proper awe
Of rank and wealth and State and law.
Nor is concealed from Britons' sight
The Germans' intellectual light,
Since Germany for many a year
Has featured the philosopher,
An object of respect colossal,
A spectacled and bearded fossil,
Generically called Strabismus,
High-Priest of *Kultur-Pessimismus*,
Who spends his conscious life entirely
In metaphysical enquiry
And purely personal pursuit
Of something called the Absolute.
The genius of the race Teutonic
Inclines, as well, to the daemonic,
Producing almost to excess
Poets distraught by storm and stress,
Who, since the first Romantic era
Have been betrothed to the Chimaera,
Enacting their subjective drama
In earth's dissolving panorama.
Works of these intellects combined
Illuminate the German mind,
As their historic annals trace
The evolution of the race,
And with such clarity define
How life is lived beyond the Rhine,
Unbiassed Britons must agree
There is no German mystery,
But from their present and their past,
Their future course may be forecast.

Does the Third Reich reincarnate
The early Teuton tribal state?
And are the Germans of our time
Like Germans in their savage prime?

The prehistoric Teuton folk,
Would never bear the tyrant's yoke,
But were of all the world's barbarians,
The most fanatic libertarians.
Administration was erratic,
But civil law was democratic
And all the bloodthirsty *élite*
As equals would in council meet.
The chieftains of the tough Teutones
Were but the first among their cronies,
And Führers in the tribal moot
Would instantly have got the boot.
Existing in a mental void,
Tumultuous freedom they enjoyed,
And their marauding lives were spent
Sans culture and enlightenment.
The savage grown sophisticated,
His love of liberty abated,
Or Germans would have been by this
As democratic as the Swiss.
Instead, the Teuton, step by step,
Discarded his primordial pep,
By lords and masters broken in
To paragons of discipline,
For despots found the German giant
Quite unexceptionably pliant —
Hence their descendants may be seen
Minced in a modern State machine.

Home life in the Hyrcynian wood
Was normal, if extremely rude,
Each Teuton in his native state,
Took to himself a female mate
(They were monogamous, though hairy,
And Teutons had no word for *fairy*)
And early tribal Teutonesses
Were greatly prized as prophetesses.
The matron sped her spouse to battle,
The maid was not the warrior's chattel,
The downfall of the German *Frau*
Occurring between then and now,
When she is only used to breed
At almost inconvenient speed.
The Teuton in his sacred groves
His captives sacrificed to droves
Of finicky divinities
Of earth and storm and wind and trees;
His gory and umbrageous rites
Attract few Third Reich proselytes,
Their purely propagandist cult
Achieving almost no result,
For Wotan's seasonal arrival
In the Wagernian revival
Wins worship merely operatic.
The modern Teuton's taste is Attic,
And since both Goth and Greek embrace
In the purged bloodstre .m of the race,
Domesticated gods of Greece
Have permits from the State police,
While human beings are sacrificed
To none except the Führer-Christ.
The Teuton's plundering expedition
Was not a civilizing mission,
Nor did his shock-troops cross the border

As harbingers of his Old Order.
His butchery was reflex action
And not a psychic satisfaction.
No *mystique* was required to toughen
The early Teuton, nature's ruffian,
And unlike his effete descendant,
He was both free and independent —
The shaggy and the shaven brute
Share nothing but their love of loot.

Have Germans souls? or must the nation
Be classified as brute creation?

While borrowing from other races
Civilization's arts and graces,
In exploration of the mind
The Germans leave the world behind;
All things which to the soul pertain
Are their peculiar domain.
And, as the pumpkin grown for prize,
Distends to quite unnatural size,
The dropsy of the German soul
Exceeds his power to control
And with its billowing contour smothers
All glimpses of the souls of others.
The German soul thus overblown,
He has too much to call his own
(In 'Faust', by Goethe, thus expressed,
'Two souls reside within my breast.')
His reason neither can supplant —
He cannot clear his mind of Kant —
But to the soul the soul must give
The crucial imperative,
Which sets it free, but in submission
To categoric intuition.

Long since have German life and letters
Repudiated reason's fetters
And with tumultuous heartbeats rent
The shackles of enlightenment,
And hailed the cult of the irrational
As something genuinely national.
The German's joy is unalloyed
When drowning in the formless void,
While nothing seems more troublesome
Than psychic equilibrium.
Him his untrammelled freedom tires
Till law directs his vast desires
As dictates of a higher will,
More clearly categoric still.
Thus the Third Reich's immense decisions
And millenarian provisions,
Its infinitely cosmic actions
Commensurate with sublime abstractions,
Seemed to conspire with destiny
To give the German soul a spree.

Have German people been reborn
Since they have Nazi livery worn?

The call to labour and to arm
Worked with the Germans like a charm;
The Leader caught the Germans' ear
By shouting what they yearned to hear.
His views (to few non-Germans laudable)
Were at all times distinctly audible,
Being hurled with such dynamic force
That he was usually hoarse.
The State officials and employers,
The bankers, traders, farmers, lawyers,
The workers and the unemployed,

Were absolutely overjoyed,
While souls of professorial girth
Inflated at the Reich's rebirth.
All Germans but the German Jews,
At his apocalyptic news
Were forthwith 'changed', like Buchman's Groupers,
Especially the young Storm Troopers.
Wild bursts of native folk-song lyrical
Proclaimed a pan-Germanic miracle,
While bosses with the workers' union
Merged in a mystical communion,
And every German he and she,
Now raised to the nobility,
Drew strength from joy and joy from toil,
Up to the eyes in blood and soil.
All felt the summons of the blood,
A mighty, though diluted, flood,
And knew an elemental urge
Towards a biologic purge,
Till a remedial convulsion
Achieved the alien strain's expulsion.
Then in the sacred racial cause,
Established by the Nürnburg Laws
And by the Reich's most high authority,
The German Jews, a small minority,
Were hounded down like rats by millions
Of most respectable civilians,
While masses, wont to spend their leisure
In gluttonous and rustic pleasure,
Found lynching, licensed by the courts,
To be the very best of sports,
And from contamination free
Shed all inferiority.
When once the Reichstag was a pyre
The Reich went like a house on fire.

The blood was purged, the books were burned,
The Germans back to nature turned,
The Leader ranted to his flock,
The folk, reborn, put back the clock.


The First Reich was the ghost of Rome,
Where Germans never were at home,
For, though they wore Rome's diadem,
She scorned to be a home for them,
But from the time of Charlemagne,
Crossed her unwelcome suzerain,
While every stabilizing plan
Came up against the Vatican.
The First Reich from the Teuton nation
Enjoyed but slight collaboration,
The Holy Roman Emperor's fiat
Invariably produced a riot,
And Princes, Bishops and Electors
Announced themselves the folk's protectors,
While everybody lent a hand
In breaking up the Fatherland.
Life in this Reich of vast pretensions
But indeterminate dimensions,
A geographical expression,
Occasioned national depression,
Until the Second Reich had won
The German's place in Europe's sun.
But when the Hohenzollern's hour
Made Germany a first-class power,
United Teutons put on weight
As subjects of an Empire State,
And every German in the street
Was raised at least by several feet.
When Bismarck's Reich was toppled down,

Together with the Prussian crown,
At this incredible reverse
Morale declined from bad to worse,
And back inside their frontiers cooped,
The Germans' soaring spirits drooped,
And all the folk began to wonder
If destiny had made a blunder.
So when the Leader's piercing scream
Announced his Greater Reich *régime*,
The moping Weimar citizen
Soared up to dazzling heights again,
And once for all, the whole community
Proclaimed indissoluble unity.
The First Reich aped a world antique,
The Third is modern and unique,
The Second was a statesman's *coup*,
The Third's a destined rendezvous.
(The Leader, at the hour of fate,
Howled at the everlasting gate,
Which with the most appalling din,
Opened to let the Germans in.)
The Third Reich is a folk concern,
Which gives the little man his turn,
The little man upon the throne,
The people come into their own.
This Reich is German handiwork
Wherein no alien traces lurk,
The monument of German taste,
With flowers of German bloodlore graced,
Where German culture holds the field,
Where German earth gives German yield,
Where livestock and the very vermin
Are certified completely German;
Where German fancy, wit and humour,
Shine in the pages of *'Der Stürmer'*,

Where youth is trained by German cannibals
To make all little Germans Hannibals
And childish voices glorify
The splendour of the German sty.
The Leader's histrionic raving
Reveals the nation's deepest craving,
Their noble greed, their holy hate,
He is themselves articulate.
The herd that on its Leader dotes
Can joyfully dispense with votes,
The crowd, transported in a fit,
Is in itself a plebiscite
And rehabilitated souls
Can spit on parliaments and polls.
The folk sees in the Leader's face
The highspot of their hero-race,
For him they joy to cast behind
The common virtues of mankind,
To sign an era with his name
That makes a glory of their shame,
And kiss the earth he treads upon —
A thing ill-favoured, but their own.
And when this German Prospero
Who made the world-wide tempest blow,
Together with his book is drowned
Deeper than e'er did plummet sound,
Plus half-a-million Calibans,
The Third Reich's picked Praetorians,
Some four-score millions will be left
Once more of leadership bereft,
In a discouraged frame of mind,
Unable their own way to find
Until another super-soul
Points to another destined goal.
Where they may build on heights sublime,

A foothold in the flux of time.
Since Germans are and always were
A race without a character,
They must behind a Leader keep
Exactly like fourfooted sheep,
A docile and sheepsheaded nation,
For ever the black sheep's temptation;
And since in triumph or disaster
A servile folk must serve a master,
And nothing can till kingdom come
Transform the soul of flunkeydom,
In Germany, once more defeated,
Past history may be repeated,
For which the world must stand prepared
When the Fourth Reich shall be declared.


## WHO SHALL WASH THE RHINE?

And can St George with one shrewd stroke,
This Dragon slay, and quell this folk?
And how will he, as Europe's saviour,
Ensure the latter's good behaviour?
While mortal combat he proclaims,
He's silent on his post-war aims,
Which waiting world and clamorous Press
Can but approximately guess.
St George preserves complete discretion
Concerning future intercession,
And at each query or suggestion
Desires due notice of the question.
For the duration of the war
Democracy's executor,
He neither takes nor gives direction
Till after the post-war election.
His past alone provides a clue

To what the Champion may do.
Be Dragons never so unsightly
He never swerves from conduct knightly,
So, to the more detached spectator,
Is not, *au fond* a Dragon hater.
(A Dragon, thoroughly redeemed,
May be an ally much esteemed,
If circumstances past surmise
Unfortunately should arise.)
And though he, too, has in his time
Counted rebellion no crime,
And Right Divine a paltry thing
When conscience stood against the King,
Since Civil War and revolution
Merely embalmed the Constitution,
Lack of political restraint
Finds little favour with the Saint.
The revolution's still to be
In European society,
And if armed combats start between
Small dragons, will he intervene,
Or after this decisive bout
Let Europe's dragons fight it out?
While ever girded for The Right,
The Champion is no simple knight,
But immemorial trustee
Of Britain's vested chivalry.
Knight of the Bath and of the Garter,
He's nothing like a Christian martyr,
And, not alone the Faith's Protector,
He is a Company Director,
Linked up with Wall Street and the City,
Which, some consider, is a pity,
And fear he will his high professions
Forswear, for he has great possessions.

Moreover, in sworn Treaties trusting,
The Saint had left his armour rusting,
And pawned estates to buy his weapons,
(As often to crusaders happens)
So coming decades may be spent
In temporary embarrassment.
Then, too, he is no longer able
To take the head of the Round Table,
Since other knights of like prestige
Have also stood the Dragon's siege;
And though prepared those knights to lead
By virtue of his simple creed —
To pay his way, live no man's debtor,
And make all other people better —
The knights, with their own codes provided
Show no ambition to be guided.
St George's world-wide realm embraces
Only the more retarded races,
Towards whom his amiable attention
Smacks of unconscious condescension,
While nations who have come of age
Resist his well-meant patronage.
St George, when he has sheathed the sword,
May don his gown and mortar-board
And British rules of conduct teach
To Germans young enough to reach;
But as he never learned to rule
Through high proficiency at school,
His eminence entirely owed
To a so-far unwritten code,
Before he can become the mental
Preceptor of the Continental,
He must reform for his own nation
His hoary plan of education,
Which, far from being learning's crown,

Has definitely broken down.
The Saint, who always looked before
He leaped, alike in peace or war,
And was habitually found
With both feet firmly on the ground,
Now anxious islanders behold
Between the new world and the old,
In doubt if he should stand aside,
Or with the Champions allied,
On their uncharted course embark,
Leaping completely in the dark.
His course the nation must determine,
And not the future of the German,
Since to our fate we hold the key,
But not to German destiny.
Henceforth, alone, St George must plan,
Not as he would, but as he can.
Or some authority abate
As one of a triumvirate.
For as he could not, to be candid,
Knock out the Dragon single-handed,
Without assistance in his quest
From Champions of the east and west,
Once they have set its victims free
They'll have as much at stake as he.
Thus the subsidiary feud
Which agitates his neighbourhood,
The hot Vansittart controversy,
Where knights no quarter give, nor mercy,
Where pleaders for forgiveness pious
Impugn their foes with vengeful bias,
While backers of the armoured fist
Flay the refined evangelist
And rend the unresponsive skies
With contradictory battle-cries,

Though giving private satisfaction,
Will not affect united action.
Be Germans' record black or grey,
It's not the question of the day,
That issue is beside the point,
For, though the time is out of joint
The world at large will not invite
St George or them to set it right.
The British Champion's admonition
Will not dictate the Reich's partition,
Nor Britain's mobilized opinion
Make Soviet peace less Carthaginian.
The nations on the Third Reich's border,
When once released from the New Order
Seek safety in a guarantee
Not from one Champion, but three
To guard them from recurrent doom
As Germans' destined living-room.
Whoever Germany 'forgive'
They will not die that she may live;
And when the Dragon bites the dust,
Impaled with many a mortal thrust,
They pray the victors will combine
To clear Reich refuse from the Rhine.
And will St George, when all is over,
Retire behind the cliffs of Dover,
Esteeming he has done his duty
In saving Empire, home and beauty,
And European tasks resign,
Or will he help to wash the Rhine?


Here stalls St George.  There rolls the Rhine,
A scowling demarcation line
That sunders Teuton regions from

The world of western Christendom,
Exuding vapours foul and rank
From rotting slime and oozy bank,
A stench so nasty, vile and strong
That none can stand the fumes for long,
But every neighbouring population
Succumbs to gradual suffocation.
This outrage on the human nose
The Third Reich waters as it flows,
Where Germans quaff its sacred wells
And do not even think it smells,
Although its odour is not known
In European lands alone,
But wafted over seven seas,
Infects the far Antipodes,
Makes English-speaking peoples ill,
And turns the stomach of Brazil,
Nay, exhalations of the Rhine
Have almost reached the Argentine.
Therefore the nations far and wide
Denouncing the unsavoury tide
As an intolerable offence
And cause of creeping pestilence
Vote by unanimous decision
For sanitary supervision
To plan perpetual ablution
And seal the fountains of pollution;
But have they made a joint design
For cleaning out the river Rhine?
Will Russia do the lion's share?
Is it America's affair?
Will seven-and-twenty States combine
To disinfect the river Rhine?
Will Dutch and Belgians living near,
Choked by the lethal atmosphere